INTO THE CITY!

THE CHALLENGE
OF URBAN MISSION

By
Edwin R. Orton

D1375471

PUBLISHED BY BIRMINGHAM CITY MISSION
126 ARDEN ROAD, ACOCKS GREEN, BIRMINGHAM,
ENGLAND B27 6AG

© 1991 Edwin R. Orton

First published in 1991
by Birmingham City Mission

All rights reserved.
No part of this publication may be reproduced or
transmitted in any form or by any means, electronic
or mechanical, including photocopy, recording, or any
information storage and retrieval system, without
permission in writing from the publisher.

ISBN 0 9518307 0 8

Produced and Printed in Great Britain by
Nuprint Ltd, Station Road, Harpenden, Herts AL5 4SE.

DEDICATION

This book is dedicated to the memory of my brother John David Orton (1931–1991) without whose help and encouragement most of the events in this book would not have taken place.

Acknowledgements

The making of this book has been a team project lasting many years. Those who have worked, prayed, given and encouraged are too numerous to mention but without them we would not have succeeded. I wish to thank especially the trustees and committee members of BCM, particularly Mrs. Erica Burrows who has been with us from the beginning. Thanks are also due to Jean Williamson (nee Robb), Alan Cutler, Jenny Moore, Pat Lambon (my present secretary) and Mark Lacey, who took most of the photographs. Special thanks to my eldest son David for his help and encouragement in editing the first draft. Chiefly I must thank my family, especially Dorothy my wife, whose sacrifice and longsuffering gave me the freedom to engage in the events recorded.

Finally, I fully acknowledge that anything worthwile that has been achieved is only by the grace of God and to Him belongs all the glory.

Contents

Foreword

ALL OVER THE WORLD, God's people are beginning to think and pray more for the cities. The population growth in the cities is staggering and the problems our cities face are sometimes overwhelming. Here is an honest and clear book about what can be done.

It has been a privilege to know Edwin and Dorothy Orton and to follow the Lord working through them from the early days of the Mission. I know many will be helped and encouraged by this book.

One of many factors that has been such a great blessing is that the Ortons and their co-workers, in the midst of such a huge task in Birmingham, have taken such a biblical and healthy interest in so many other parts of the world. They have given time to visit and minister in other countries besides being involved in their city.

George Verwer,
International Director,
Operation Mobilisation

Introduction

HALF OF THE WORLD'S population now live in cities. In the 1980s one billion people moved from rural to urban areas. Another billion will move in the 1990s. These movements create enormous problems, but they also present tremendous opportunities. Most people move to the cities because of poverty. They seek a better standard of living, but usually they become worse off. However, they cannot go back. Often they have sold their property in the country, but the money gained is soon spent because of the high cost of living in the city.

World cities are growing at an ever increasing rate. Mexico City, with its population of twenty-three million, is growing at the rate of one million each year. Two million homeless children live on its streets. In the three largest cities of the world, 45 per cent live in appalling slums. Most people, throughout the world, face an urban future.

Changes in lifestyle for new city-dwellers present exciting possibilities for the spread of the gospel. Such people are open to new ideas and willing to make new relationships. They are often lonely and need befriending. Living in an urban area makes them much more accessible than they were in a sprawling rural district. Generally they are more receptive; they appreciate visits to their poor homes and are willing to join new churches.

City evangelism is always costly to the people who are willing to get involved. Effectiveness can only be achieved by workers living among the people they wish to reach. Their families also must pay the price of living in poor housing in the inner city, with its attendant pressures of noise, dirt, violence and crime. The education and social development of their children is greatly threatened. As a result there is a dearth of workers available for urban evangelism.

It is clear from the Bible that God has always had a concern for the cities. From the beginning such concentrations of humanity became cesspools of depravity meriting destruction. In the case of the cities of Sodom and Gomorrah, God inspired Abraham to intercede for their deliverance, although this proved to be in vain because too few righteous people lived within them.

Later, in the case of Nineveh, God sent His reluctant servant Jonah to warn of imminent judgement. That vast Assyrian capital was brought to its knees in repentance by the stern preaching of the awesome man of God. God is not willing that any should perish but that all should come to repentance. He is ever merciful and looks upon the cities with compassion.

Nowhere is this more clear than when Jesus looked on the city of Jerusalem. In AD 70 it fell to the Romans. There was no hope; the city had rejected its only Saviour.

God still has a concern for the cities of the world. Today there are cities much larger than Nineveh or Jerusalem. They contain millions of people and are still growing rapidly. Each city contains a vast heap of suffering humanity. Cities have always become centres of greed and lust. They have attracted the proud, the ambitious, the lonely and the destitute. On one hand there is wealth and waste; on the other there is poverty and need.

City missions have been working against this background since the early nineteenth century. David Nasmith began the first city mission in Glasgow in 1826. Then he moved to Dublin to start one there. Later he crossed the Atlantic, carrying the city mission message to America, where a number were founded. When he returned to Europe he was responsible for starting a mission in Paris. Then he founded the great London City Mission in 1835. Following some difference of opinion there he travelled north, originating missions in many towns and cities in England and Scotland. It was while travelling to start another mission in Guildford that he became fatally ill. He died at the age of forty.

Nasmith had accomplished a life-work of incalculable value. Many of his missions are still active. Their histories are amazing records of rescuing people of all ages, occupations and social classes from the consequences of sin and degradation. Today the vision of city mission has developed and spread. The great Berlin City Mission celebrated a hundred years of service in 1977. Such institutions are common throughout Europe. But they are also a great power for good in North America, Africa and Australia.

The work has always been that of telling and caring. In Glasgow the objective had been to tell everyone about Christ, especially the poor. This entailed a programme of systematic visitation of homes for the purpose of leaving a Bible in each one. But the physical and social needs were so great that the missionaries found it necessary to do something about these as well. So they opened 'Ragged Schools' to educate the illiterate. They provided free medicine through their dispensaries. Food, clothing and fuel were given to the very poor. Petty criminals were represented in the courts and their families aided when heavy, unjust sentences were applied. The court missionaries did their work so well that our modern probationary service is rooted in it.

But the message of the gospel has been the prime concern. 'To reach the unreached' in the cities has always been the aim. Several generations of men and women have laboured consistently to realise that vision. It has taken them into millions of homes of every kind. Prisons, hospitals, factories and markets have also become regular mission fields. Thousands of lives have been changed. Their true stories of drama, pathos and humour are already on record.

The city missions are therefore an integral part of the Christian life of the nation. They pioneered the movement towards interdenominational co-operation while not compromising their evangelical theology. Many crusades, celebrations and movements have come and gone. The city mission's work is long-term, stable, constant and wide-reaching in its influence.

There had been a Birmingham City Mission before we began the work of the new Birmingham City Mission, or rather a Birmingham Town Mission, because when it started in 1837 Birmingham did not have city status. It became a city in 1889. The mission had been founded by David Nasmith on the same lines as the London City Mission. It grew into a thriving concern which played an important role in the city's life for over eighty years. During that period it ran several mission centres, with Sunday services attended by hundreds of people. It had two refuge homes for women, which were responsible for reclaiming hundreds of lives from prostitution. The mission agents visited thousands of homes in the most needy areas of the city. Special work was done among cabmen and also among the deaf and dumb. This admirable mission finally closed in 1924. Records of its activities still exist but they were completely unknown to us when we first started.

Today the need for city missions is as great as ever. This book is written to encourage interest in this vital work.

Much of the material recorded is autobiographical. It is included not for self-advertisement but to serve as a modern example of how a city mission has been started and developed by those who had nothing but a little faith in a great God. If this inspires others to follow, it will be well worth the writer's effort.

1

A Mission on My Conscience

'SIR, THERE'S SOME MEN here to see you!' The boy's voice called across the noisy, crowded club-room. It was a Monday evening in October 1965. The boisterous lads had taken a lot of energy from me. I had already spent a day teaching in the boy's secondary school so any excuse to stop and rest was welcome.

'Could you take over, Skip?' I asked. 'Skipper' David Torpey, with whom I shared leadership of the boys' group, little knew how significant that remark would prove to be.

There were five men at the door, only one known to me. They had been attending a meeting in the city centre and afterwards talked together of the spiritual needs of Britain's second city, Birmingham. 'What we need is a city mission,' said one. In the ensuing discussion my name was mentioned as one who had a special interest in the subject. The man who knew me suggested that they come to see me. Here they were.

No plans for a takeover

Before moving to Birmingham in 1961 my wife and I had been living and working in Essex. There we had planted a church on a large new housing estate. We had also come into contact with the London City Mission. Their missionary at Tilbury was T.E. Bugby, who served the seamen in that part of London and spoke Arabic and several Asian languages. From time to time I visited the ships with him and he often suggested I joined the LCM. That was far from my mind. I was not interested in city missions. When he heard I was leaving for Birmingham he asked me to look out for 'his men'—the Asian seamen who jumped ship and moved to the Midlands. 'They could do with a city mission there,' he urged.

Just before we left Essex another friend had given me a newsletter headed 'Birmingham City Mission'. This was an interesting discovery and I promised to visit the mission on my arrival. Three weeks later I was there, talking to Winifred Hellmuth and Ruth Bourne in their premises in Upper Gough Street. The city council had let two houses to them for their work. Because of redevelopment they were being moved to Mary Street, Balsall Heath. This was in Birmingham's 'red light' district, and also in the midst of a large Asian population. It was ideal for mission work. However, there were problems. This kind of work attracts special Satanic pressures and often suffers casualties. Only a few weeks later Miss Hellmuth called at my house. In a state of real distress she thrust a file of papers at me. 'That is the Birmingham City Mission,' she cried, 'now it is your responsibility.'

At this time I was in no position to take on so great a task. My wife and I were just settling in our new home and a new baby had arrived, making us the parents of four children. The home was the focal point of the new church which we were planting. Sunday school, Bible classes, prayer meetings, youth activities and worship meetings were all held in the home which God had given us. In addition, I was teaching religious education to over 400 boys in school. No, I was in no position to lead a city mission. Also, there was quite a lot of bad feeling about the work in Balsall Heath. There were debts to clear and the mission houses were returned to the city council. A number of people felt hurt. This was no good foundation on which to build. There I let the matter rest.

God, on the other hand, was not going to let it rest, or rather, let me rest.

Two years went by and still the mission was on my conscience. Those two women had made great steps of faith. Their hearts were right and they had done an important work. Had it all been in vain? Would no one else take up the burden to reach the lost for Christ in the needy inner city? Eventually I could stand it no more, I had to act. The trouble had been that the ladies had not had the backing of Christian leaders. They had not understood the need for trustees, auditors, management committees and the like. If a new city mission were to succeed we must start there. I decided to enlist the interest of clergymen, pastors, and Christian businessmen. My aim was to get them interested and then leave them to organise the mission. I had no intention of being more involved myself.

Soon discouragement set in. There were few replies to my letters, and those which came were rather negative. A few people were willing to see me. They listened patiently and then poured out their stories of overwork, frustration and inability to take on anything else. Some were clearly not impressed with me, and had no idea what a city mission was or could be. I returned home baffled and discouraged. But I took the matter to the Lord. I told Him that I had done all I could. Besides, I was already over-committed myself. If He wanted me to be involved in a city mission, He would have to come and get me. At that point He did. 'Sir, there's some men here to see you!'

2

The First Years

THE FIRST MINUTED meeting of the present BCM is dated 29 November 1965. It was held in our family home on the Kingshurst estate. Fifteen people were present. Each was active in some Christian work around the city. They came from eight different districts, from different denominations and races. After introductions I presented to them the needs of the city, the scope of a city mission and the steps which could be taken to found one. At the conclusion it was decided that we should go ahead immediately to prepare for this great work.

There were many practical problems, especially that of communication. We had no telephone. When we applied for one, lines were in such short supply that we had to wait over two years before one was installed. We had no car. All our travelling had to be done by bus. Even letter writing was difficult because we possessed no typewriter or duplicator. No money was available to buy them.

Prayer was given a high priority. We knew we could not succeed by ourselves. God alone could see us through. Each meeting was primarily devoted to prayer. Business meetings and prayer meetings were held monthly. God began to answer. Small sums of money started to arrive and soon we had our typewriter.

No coincidence

As the correspondence grew, cardboard boxes appeared in our dining room. Dorothy, my wife, although very patient, began to complain. 'You can't keep all these papers here, you'll need a cupboard to put them in.' 'Yes,' I thought, ' I need a filing cabinet.' I heard there was a shop in Broad Street which specialised in second-hand office furniture. I went to have a look around and saw just the cabinet I needed. It had four drawers, was made of steel, and was dark green with brown handles. I could afford it, but only just, and it did seem expensive. I looked at it, opened the drawers, thought about it and prayed about it. Then I left the shop, walked up the street, came back again and had another look. I almost decided to buy it but finally left, returning home to give the matter more thought.

It was tea time when I arrived home, and I had just sat down to eat when the doorbell rang. At the door was Alan Fleming, a Christian builder and member of the BCM committee. He knew nothing about our need or my trip to town. 'Could you do with a filing cabinet?' he asked. 'We were demolishing a building today and came across a good one. Rather than throw it away I thought maybe you could use it.'

There it was on his car roof-rack. It was identical to the one which an hour earlier I had been inspecting. Had I bought it, it would have been delivered later. This one had arrived immediately—free of charge. Today it is still in use in our general offices.

Into battle

By March 1966 it was decided that we should begin the work of evangelism. One Saturday evening a small group of committee members and friends held BCM's first open-air meet-

ing in the Bull Ring. This place has traditionally been Birmingham's speakers' corner. John Wesley once preached
there. Many others had followed but in early post-war years
the area had been completely redeveloped. When the work
was completed the former generation of open-air preachers
had passed and no one seemed ready to begin again. So,
here we were on a cold, blustery March evening, feebly
trying. It rained. We stood under the newly constructed
Ringway and preached to the few passers-by. Some listened.
One woman became a Christian that night.

Saturday nights are not the best times for open-air meetings. Often we were surrounded by abusive drunks or party
revellers. Sometimes we were shouted down. It was decided
that the first piece of equipment we should buy was a public
address amplifier. This was heavy and had to be carried and
taken by bus to the city. Opposition came from the police.
Although no one resided in the vicinity, and we could hardly
be heard above the noise of the traffic, they claimed that
complaints had been made. We stood our ground regarding
our rights for free speech. They countered by invoking a law
which prevented the use of loudspeakers after 9 pm—a law
which had been passed to prevent ice-cream vendors distur-
bing children's sleep in residential areas. The battle had
begun.

'Welcome to Castle Vale'

Our next move was to commence door-to-door visitation on
the new housing estates. A large one, called Castle Vale, was
being constructed on the east side. As people moved into
their new homes so we called offering them gospels and New
Testaments. The people were not hospitable and we found
no practising Christians ready to welcome us. It was many
months before a home was opened to us and meetings
started.

Words of encouragement

In May 1966 we held our first conference, at the 'Gaines' in Worcestershire. Feeling our need for help in advancing the new mission, we had approached the London City Mission and they sent us a senior missionary, G.H. Davies, to be our speaker. He greatly encouraged us. About thirty people gathered for the weekend to pray, learn of the work of other city missions and hear the Word of God. We were on holy ground and we knew it. Great was our joy and excitement.

Switching on the radio by chance one day I had heard a man telling of his ministry in Liverpool. The programme was run by Eric Hutchings, the evangelist. I wrote to him and he became a firm supporter of the BCM. He also put me in touch with the speaker, Mr H.G. Bogle, of the Liverpool City Mission. He was unable to attend our conference but sent a tape with a special message of encouragement.

The wider world

That summer World Cup football came to England. When we heard that matches would be played in Birmingham's Villa Park we planned some evangelism. The teams came from Germany and Spain. We obtained literature in the languages of the competing countries and distributed it among the crowds of supporters. Aston Park was turned into a German Biergarten. Outreach was continued later at night among the revellers. The BCM had taken its first steps to being involved in world outreach.

It seemed to us that progress was slow. Our small team of voluntary workers were spending at least one day per month evangelising, in addition to the weekly open-air meetings. We longed for full-time workers but knew that much founda-tional work still needed to be done. Someone suggested that we needed £100 in the bank before we employed anyone. Our total income up to 30 September was £102.17. More support was needed so efforts were made to enlist a body of prayer partners.

A look behind closed doors

The official inaugural meeting of the BCM took place on 22 October 1966. It was held in the Friends' Meeting House and was attended by over 200 people from about 50 different churches of various denominations. Stanley Seymour brought greetings and shared experiences of the London City Mission. The main speaker was the Revd George Whyte, Superintendent of the Liverpool City Mission. He described an outwardly prosperous city but looked behind the closed doors, as God did, at the sin, violence, loneliness, grief and need of the people inside. Only the good news of Christ could bring peace and true happiness to those in need. We had to take that news to the people where they were, in their homes and on the streets.

At that time the country was numb from the Aberfan disaster. In that small Welsh mining town a school filled with children had been engulfed by a landslide from a coal tip. Many children died but some were rescued by volunteers working feverishly with bare hands. The tragedy was mentioned in our inaugural meeting, and we stood in silence remembering that sorrowing community, the bereaved and the injured. It was significant to us that we were launching a rescue mission of even greater urgency and with far-reaching implications.

'As a little child'

'Don't talk to me about God, I come from Aberfan!' The young Welshman bitterly heckled the speaker in the Bull Ring open-air meeting. Clearly he was full of anger and resentment. After speaking publicly the preacher approached him personally. 'I was one of those who tried to save the schoolchildren,' the Welshman continued. 'How can there be a God of love when you find the child of a friend buried alive in sludge from the tip?'

It was a hard question to answer. Gradually the whole question of suffering was discussed, leading to the suffering of Christ upon the cross.

The man was clutching a large parcel. Opening it he said, 'Look at this. I painted it myself.' It was the portrait of a child crying. The preacher begged to borrow it for a while. Back on the rostrum he held it for all to see and preached a sermon on the text, 'Except you become as a little child and be converted, you cannot enter God's kingdom.' Gently he explained to the crowd how the picture came to be painted, then he handed it back to the artist.

Three weeks later at the usual time for the meeting it was pouring with rain. Unable to preach, the workers were content to give out tracts to people sheltering in shop doorways. The preacher felt a tap on his shoulder and looking round he recognised the Welshman. He was smiling broadly. 'I'm glad you are here,' he said, 'I came specially to see you. I've been converted and have become a Christian, and I wanted you to know.'

3

No 36—A Place of Our Own

'NO, LORD, NOT THIS PLACE!' I was looking at the heaps of rubbish and obvious signs of the local rat population. Surely we could find a better place than this.

Each time we went to our Bull Ring meetings we were accosted by people asking for money. They were always down on their luck. 'Give me the price of a cup of tea and a sandwich,' they would say. At first we would give them a little cash. Then we realised that the drink they wanted was not necessarily tea! 'If only we had a place to take them,' we sighed. It would also save aching arms if we didn't need to heave equipment on and off buses. We had looked everywhere for a place to rent. Now we had found one—but what a mess!

It is amazing what a change can be made by a team of eager youngsters armed with soap and water, and large tins of paint. The colour scheme was blue and white because they are the colours of Birmingham Football Club. Their stadium is called St Andrew's, after the church next door. Hence the fisherman's blue and the saintly white. This point was not lost on the preacher, who was often surrounded by local football fans!

There were bars at the large windows of our new BCM home. We joked that some of our clients would feel at home if we left them there. But we could do with some curtains to hide them. Money was scarce, the windows were large and curtains expensive. Visiting two elderly ladies one day, I overheard them say that their missionary sewing group had been given some curtain material. I told them the size, amount and colour of what I was looking for. Shortly afterwards a large parcel arrived. What they had been given was exactly the size and amount I had specified. And they were blue and white!

The owner of 36 Bromsgrove Street, our new premises, was a businessman who liked to make money. After letting us the ground-floor room behind his shop he insisted we hired the room above, which doubled the rent. He also urged us to buy the existing gas heaters, which later we learned he had sold to the previous occupants too! However, this 'long room' was to prove invaluable. To begin with, it contained an enormous table which, when cut up, was exactly the size required for partitioning the room below.

We obtained our base in 1968. That year, Gordon Sitch, fresh from Bible College, became our first full-time worker. Jean Robb also joined us, as a voluntary worker. She was a young teacher, who eventually became our full-time secretary. All kinds of people were drawn to the place. The vagrants who accosted us in the streets now came to our rooms regularly. Our work among the homeless was taking shape.

Tommy's turnaround

Tommy was brought to us during our Tuesday open-air meeting. He was dirty and in rags and was clutching a bottle of methylated spirits. That first encounter ended with him being arrested and taken to Digbeth Police Station. Some days later he arrived at No. 36 a changed man. He had a remarkable story of the way God had spoken to him when he was in a pub. The Word of God had come clearly to his mind. He had run out of the bar and become completely sober, losing his desire for drink. His one topic of conversation became the Bible. Previously this Irishman had been in and out of prison on almost every charge, including manslaughter. He told us that he had been arrested seventy times for being drunk and disorderly, thirty-five times in his own name and thirty-five in other people's, including Winston Churchill!

Jimmy—the con man

Jimmy was an even worse case, not so much a drunk as a hardened criminal. One day he arrived just as we were leaving. As usual he asked for money. We refused, but as he was clearly hungry and we had no food he was taken to a local cafe. Indicating that he should sit down, the situation was quietly explained to the waitress. She failed to understand. 'The man at the back of the room is a "down-and-out", I whispered. 'Please give him food to the value of this money.' Jimmy heard. 'I'm not a down-and-out,' he boomed, 'I'm a burglar!'

Some weeks later we were having a night of prayer in our meeting room. Quite late someone joined the group praying. His heavy breathing and the strong smell of alcohol caused me to look up. It was Jimmy. I began to pray aloud for him. He had recently committed despicable crimes against innocent people. We prayed that this wicked man might turn to God in repentance. 'I'm not as bad as that!' he cried. Perhaps that is why he didn't change. He conned everyone else and he thought he could con God.

With matrimony in mind!

Prayer has been an essential part of the mission from its beginning. Now that we had a place of our own it became a house of prayer. Sometimes we would spend a whole day or night in prayer. God answered in wonderful ways. There were also interesting spin-offs.

During one of these nights of prayer we were joined by a young clergyman. Unknown to us he had a special request. His church was in a poor area of the city and many of his parishioners suffered from marital problems. Being single he felt unable to help as he should. He began to pray for a wife. He attended our prayer meeting on his fifth day of fasting and prayer. During the meeting a young woman entered whom he had never seen before. Somehow he knew that this was the person God had for him but before he had the opportunity to speak to her she left. He had no idea who she was or where she came from. The following day he was on a bus, heading home, when he suddenly remembered he needed to buy a birthday card. Immediately he got off the bus and returned to the local Christian bookshop. He arrived at the same time as another customer—the lady he had seen in the prayer meeting. Soon after, there was a wedding to celebrate.

The new evangelistic centre attracted all kinds of people. Among them was a young couple, who had run away from their parents in Northern Ireland. They were desperately in need, hungry, homeless and with no clothing other than what they had on. And the girl was pregnant. Mission personnel counselled and cared for them. Soon they heard the good news of Jesus—of His forgiveness and their need of repentance—and believed it. As a first step they realised their need to get married. This was arranged at the local Registry Office. Peter Skinner, the missionary who had brought them to Christ, acted as best man and I acted as the bride's father! Although now legally married, the young woman was unhappy. She had wanted a church wedding. An approach was made to the young clergyman who met his wife-to-be in our all-night prayer meeting and he agreed to allow his church to be used for a service of blessing for the newly-weds. A group of people came from my own church to form the congregation and a Christian marriage service was conducted. The wedding party then returned to our Bromsgrove Street centre where the church members had laid on a reception, which even included a wedding cake! What a wonderful change had taken place in this destitute couple since they found Christ at the BCM centre.

Down Alleluia Alley

For four years the centre was the mission headquarters. It had its limitations, chiefly no street frontage, except for a small gate. This opened into a long alley-way, at the bottom of which was our building. The young people nicknamed it 'Alleluia Alley'! The main attraction for us was its central position. From there we could walk to our open-air meetings or reach out to shoppers, theatre-goers, market workers, and travellers using the main railway and coach stations. It was also easy to find, and many people succeeded in doing so!

In 1972 the shop in front of the centre became vacant and the BCM was able to obtain the lease. Soon the ground floor was being used as a coffee bar, bookshop, office, doctor's surgery and counselling centre. Above that we had a prayer room and library, while the second floor served as my office. Now that we had direct access to the street even more people dropped in to see us.

The Chinese community

'Do you believe in healing?' The speaker was a small young Chinese man. 'Yes,' I replied, 'I believe in a God who can heal. What is your problem?' He looked very sad as he said, 'It's my wife, she's had an accident on the motorway. Her neck is broken and she is completely paralysed.'

There in the shop we stood and prayed for this young
Chinese man, his critically injured wife and his three small
children. After praying for her I asked if I could visit the lady
in hospital. I thought she would be in one of the Birmingham
hospitals. But I was wrong. I was told she was in the Stoke
Manderville Paraplegic Hospital in Aylesbury. It was a long
way to go, but later I did, and, after succeeding visits saw this
Chinese lady, Mary Tan, put her trust in Jesus. Physically
she was helpless. The only muscles she could move were
those of her face. Speech was difficult because she could only
breathe with the aid of an artificial respirator. However, she
learned to pray and then to smile. Having become a Christian she also became my prayer partner.

Another surprise came when I asked the husband if I
could visit him and the children in their home, thinking they
would live in one of the Birmingham suburbs. In fact they
lived in Liverpool. This took me on another long journey. It
also led to a difficult situation in the Chinese underworld. Mr
Tan was a compulsive gambler who was in great debt and
evil men were pressurising him. So a visit to his bank manager was arranged, which proved helpful. We were also able
to put him in touch with local Christians who cared for him
and the children.

Bromsgrove Street is the centre of Birmingham's large
Chinese community. The area contains not only many Chinese restaurants, but also warehouses and stores which supply Chinese businesses throughout the country. Many
Chinese people entered our doors. Many also went next
door—a recreation centre—to play table tennis. This was a
centre for Communist propaganda. At that time Chairman
Mao's *Little Red Book* was very popular. To counter this
propaganda we distributed copies of God's book in Chinese.

There are many Christians among the Chinese people. As
the community was concerned to teach their children the
Chinese language and culture they asked to use our centre as
a Saturday school. For several years it served as such. What

a joy it was to see our building packed with Chinese people on parents' day as we showed Christian films and preached the gospel to them.

Exemption granted

The extension of our premises brought greater financial burdens. A demand for rates amounting to £500 caused us to call a special prayer meeting. There we were joined by a Christian man who was a stranger to us. At the end of the meeting he told us he had not felt free to pray as he did not think we should pay rates at all.

After making some enquiries for us he stated that we would be exempt from rates if we were a registered place of worship, which we were not. The building was officially described as a shop, warehouse and factory.

'What do you do in this room?' he asked. We were standing in the large room at the back of the building. I explained that it was used for our homeless men. We fed them and allowed them to sit in the warm while we showed films. At nine o'clock each evening we held an evangelistic service. 'Do you mean that you preach and pray in this room every day?' 'Yes, of course.' 'Then surely this is more of a place of worship than most churches which are only open on Sundays?' As we moved around the building we told him of the other spiritual uses made of the property—nights of prayer, Bible studies, counselling and teaching sessions.

With this information he approached the authorities. A plan was submitted to the Registrar General and from that day no rates were payable. God had provided again.

Visitors from overseas

Men and women of many nations, races and languages have come to our mission. A young motor-cyclist arrived one morning. He said he had been driving past when he noticed the Bible text displayed. This compelled him to stop and come inside. 'It is exactly one year ago that I became a Christian,' he confessed, 'but I have not been following the Lord as I should. The text challenged me to seek help.' He was counselled and encouraged to renew his commitment to Christ. When asked how he came to be passing he said he was on a world tour and just happened to come by. 'Where have you come from?' I asked. 'From New Zealand. My father is Chinese and my mother is Maori!'

A frequent visitor to the mission has been an elderly man from the Ukraine. He has appreciated Scripture given to him in his own language, but he has valued more the friendship and warmth of our welcome. During World War II he was pressed into forced labour by the Germans, who invaded his country. At the end of the war he fled to the West because he had no home and did not wish to live under Communism. After many horrific adventures he arrived in England as a refugee. In great poverty he lived alone in a decrepit house. But he is a devout Christian. Gradually we were able to help him, in spite of language difficulties, to become a British citizen, obtain a passport and travel to America to visit his one remaining relative.

Another Eastern European used to frequent our open-air meetings in the Bull Ring. Usually he was the worse for drink. He was a Communist and an atheist. Often he would heckle the preacher and make a nuisance of himself. One day he happened to be passing our mission centre just as I opened the door. He was sober and he stopped to talk. Though I listened carefully I could not place his accent. 'Where do you come from?' I asked. 'I am from Lithuania,' was his reply. Asking him to wait a moment I went inside and looked through our supply of foreign literature. He was amazed and beamed with pleasure when I returned and gave him a Gospel of John in the Lithuanian language.

Some weeks later I saw this formerly aggressive atheist walking in the city centre. I asked him how he was getting on with his book. He put his hands together and said reverently, 'I read it every day.'

Many Asians frequent the market place adjoining St Martin's in the Bull Ring so I asked the rector for permission to use the notice-board outside the church to display a scripture poster in Hindi. He agreed, and as I put up the poster I realised that two Indian gentlemen were watching. I asked them if they could read the words, as I couldn't. They kindly obliged and this led to an in-depth conversation on the meaning of the Bible text. Then I asked one of the men which part of Birmingham he lived in, thinking he would say Sparkbrook or Aston. He replied that he didn't live in Birmingham but Bradford and that he was here just to meet his friend. Turning to him I asked the same question, only to be told that he didn't live in Birmingham either but had just arrived at the airport on a flight from Delhi!

On one occasion a young black man came into our bookshop and I overheard him saying that he was in trouble and needed help. At first I thought he was a local West Indian looking for work but on further inquiry he told me his story. He was a Muslim from West Africa but was studying chemistry in Moscow University, Russia! During his vacation he had made his way to Britain to visit relatives, travelling overland by rail to Ostend and then by sea to Harwich. In London he had his baggage stolen, including money, his rail ticket to Harwich and sea ticket to Ostend. Fortunately he had on his person his rail ticket to Moscow. In Birmingham his relatives had treated him badly, and he found himself with no money and no work permit. As he still had three weeks of his vacation left we suggested that he did some voluntary work in our hostel for homeless people, where he too would be cared for. If he was generally useful we would reward him with a gift—we could not employ him. So at the end of the time we bought him the tickets necessary for him to get back to Russia. But while he was with us we introduced him to our missionary from Nigeria, Paul Olise, who took him home and eventually led him to Christ. How thrilled we were in due course to receive a letter from Moscow telling of this student's growth in Christ and that he was meeting with other Christians.

Not guilty of murder

It would be good if we could say that every day people were converted in the Bromsgrove Street centre but that was not the case; much of the work was routine and mundane. Nevertheless there was a consistent witness, people were cared for and attention was given to keeping records. This was just as well for at least one man.

Among the regular attenders at the soup kitchen in the 'room at the back' were two drinking friends. One was a resident of our hostel in Granville Street, the other of the Salvation Army hostel in Snow Hill. When the body of the latter was found in a derelict house in Winson Green our man was arrested and charged with his murder.

Fortunately Margaret Anderson, our staff member in charge of the men's work at the time, had kept careful records. She was able to prove that the victim had attended the soup kitchen in good health after the two men had been fighting, and therefore the blows exchanged were not the direct cause of his death. Margaret worked hard on this case, attending the court on several occasions until our man was acquitted.

Then followed the matter of the dead man's funeral. He had no relatives and few friends. It became the BCM director's responsibility to conduct the service at the Uplands Cemetery in Smethwick. Four men from the mission were present, including the man who had been accused of his murder. There followed a long period of rehabilitation for this man, who was a confirmed alcoholic, but finally he became a Christian and was employed by another organisation caring for the homeless.

4

A Birmingham 'Message'—By Phone

I T WAS A BEAUTIFUL, sunny May afternoon as we
looked across the city. Harold Bogle, a short, elderly,
sharp-witted preacher from Liverpool, stood with me. He
had come specially from his busy city mission schedule to
visit the newly fledged society in Birmingham. Now he
wanted a panoramic view of the large West Midland con-
urbation, and there was only one place for that. Few local
people managed to achieve it but we did. We were standing
on the balcony of the Rotunda building, the tall round office
block on the city's highest point overlooking the Bull Ring
and St Martin's Church.

To the north we could see the heights of Barr Beacon, the
wooded hills of Cannock Chase and to the right the large
expanse of Sutton Coldfield's park. Westward lay Clent
Hills, hiding from us the historic town of Kidderminster.
These high spots of English beauty divert the eye from the
ugly remains of the Industrial Revolution known appropri-
ately as the Black Country.

Southward we viewed the rich farmlands of Worcestershire. On the city's edge lay the Lickey Hills, beneath
which sprawls the great Longbridge motor factory. To the

left, as we looked, were the ever growing suburbs, reaching into Warwickshire and Shakespeare country. The quietness had gone. We became aware of the distant roar of traffic from the congested motorways which surround the city.

Here was a modern metropolis, Britain's second largest city, rapidly changing in an economic boom, but altering too in culture and religion with the influx of multitudes from the Indian sub-continent and other distant lands.

Harold Bogle knew too much of city life to be beguiled by splendid architecture, industrial magnificence or the materialistic credit card culture of the modern shopping precinct. This was a city of people—boys and girls, men and women, old and young. All had a need for God. Ways and means must be found to reach them with the good news of Jesus. 'Why not use the telephone?' he suggested. 'Many of these folks will not attend church and it will take a long time to visit all the homes.'

During the succeeding months the idea grew. Among a parcel of secondhand books received from America was a work entitled, *God Gave Me a Telephone*. A pastor described vividly the exciting opportunities he had of counselling people of all kinds over the telephone.

Then we heard of the interest of Norah Coggan, the sister of the then Archbishop of Canterbury. She was using the newly developed telephone answering machines to provide an anonymous service of spiritual help. An invitation was given to her to come to Birmingham and tell of her new ministry, which she simply called 'Message'.

In December 1969 the Birmingham Christian Telephone Service opened with a call taken by the Lord Mayor at the launch in Dr Johnson House. The equipment was housed at the BCM Bromsgrove Street centre. A group of clergymen and other leaders, led by the Revd David MacInnes of St Philip's Cathedral, provided most of the messages.

The system was simple. A short message from the Bible was recorded on the answering machine. At the end of the message another number was given so that the caller could ring and have a live conversation with a counsellor if desired. The service was advertised in the press and by other means. It had the attraction that the caller remained anonymous and that the message could be heard at any time. During the first year of operation 30,000 calls were received. A small percentage of callers then rang the counsellors, who were on duty in their own homes. These callers were not only from the Birmingham area but from as far away as Scotland and the South. Many were elderly, lonely or distressed people. But there were also city business people, night workers in factories, office workers and even children in need. Free literature was sent. Some callers were visited, others were put in touch with churches local to them and still others were referred to Bromsgrove Street.

Message received

One lady received a tract in the street. She read it with interest and noticed the 'Message' service number stamped on the back. That day's message was so applicable to her as she listened that she called the counsellor. He suggested she visit the Bromsgrove Street centre. There she was helped to make her commitment to Christ. As she was about to leave the centre—now a Christian—she met the person who had given her the tract. The distributors had just returned.

'May I write an article about your telephone service?' The speaker was a farmer's wife. Two years earlier a terrible tragedy had occurred in her life. Her little boy had been killed in a road accident in the lane outside their farm. In her distress someone had told her about our telephone service. She told us that she had been ringing daily since then. The Word of God had done its work in her heart. Now she wanted others to know and was asking permission to write an article in a farmers' magazine.

Callers anonymous

God alone knows the stories of the many thousands of callers who have remained anonymous. During the time that the mission was setting out, with few full-time staff, this service was particularly important. It was a means of reaching the unreached using available resources of money and man-power. All the workers were volunteers.

After the second year the founding group felt unable to continue, chiefly for financial reasons. They had borrowed money and were without cash to repay their loan, even after approaching churches and engaging in fund-raising activities. So in 1972 the mission agreed to be solely responsible for the service and to pay for it from money received in answer to prayer. Since then there have been no appeals for money and all bills have been paid.

Work of this nature is bound to have problems and we certainly had our share. Many of these arose because of the limited time available for counselling and the location of the equipment. Ideally we would have had a twenty-four hour manned service, but because we lacked the staff to do that the time for live counselling was confined to the evenings. At the end of each recorded message we used to say, 'If you would like to talk to someone please ring (and we would quote the number of the duty counsellor) between 8 and 10 pm.' As the counsellors differed from day to day it was necessary to make each new recording after 10 pm, which meant a late visit to the centre. Bromsgrove Street is in the heart of the market area so at night there was a likelihood of being confronted with unsavoury characters, or even rats!

Answering machines were new to the telephone service. The law did not allow private machines to be plugged into the system, therefore GPO engineers were called upon. Their machines operated a reel-to-reel loop system which was new to them as well as to us. After a while we knew more about the recorders than they did! When a fault arose and a new engineer called we spent time explaining to him how the equipment worked before he tried to repair it.

Everyone was relieved when the 'Message' Christian Telephone Service was moved to the new church at Kingshurst. We obtained new machines operated with cassettes, and a new telephone number—770 6000—which was easy to remember. It made a pleasant change to record the message in a clean room furnished with modern equipment.

The new building had a comfortable lounge which provided us with the opportunity to invite all the helpers and new recruits to training sessions. Scripts had to be written for the recorded messages. They needed to be topical, up to date, interesting and concise. Care was necessary regarding the language used and, of course, the Christian message had to be clearly presented.

Training was also given in the vocal presentation, ensuring a cheerful, friendly, confident quality which minimised the sense that the message was a recording. Counsellors also needed training so they could encourage the shy and fearful to open up and share their problems. It takes special skill to respect a caller's desire for anonymity yet inspire confidence so that he or she can be really helped. How wonderful if such a caller can be led to Christ.

Some callers used this service daily, therefore a programme of progressive Christian teaching was planned. Carefully chosen Bible texts were entered on the calendar for each day and scriptwriters used them as the basis for their messages.

Answering a need

One regular caller known to us suffered from agoraphobia. She dialled and listened anonymously for months before she found the courage to speak to a counsellor. Only after many conversations would she give personal details about herself. When she did, someone called several times and then took her outside her home for the first time in years. Eventually the lady became a regular member of a local church, over-came her agoraphobia and saw her husband converted too.

Perhaps it was because the service was advertised by means of car stickers, as well as posters and the local press, that a city gentleman called us. He was in great distress and needed careful counselling. As he talked he kept putting more money in the pay phone. There was a lot of background noise, and when asked he said he was ringing from Liverpool Street Railway Station in London, more than a hundred miles away.

Another rang from Lancashire. He told us that he was director of a large office near Preston. One of his secretaries had been asked to ring a business number but had misdialled and accidentally come across our 'Message'. She was so interested that she had dialled again and got all the other girls in the office to listen. The director was a Christian, and was so pleased to see what a good impression the message had made in the office that he telephoned the counselling number to encourage us by telling us what had been happening.

Many callers felt very much alone because of a recent bereavement or a broken marriage. Some were suicidal, and it is quite possible that lives were saved because of the service. How worthwhile it was to read the Scriptures and to pray with such people over the telephone. Occasionally one would ring again a few days later to thank us for the help that had been given in their time of desperation.

5

Inservice Training

GEORGE STEPHENSON, JAMES WATT and Matthew Boulton will be remembered for ever for their vital part in industrial history. Their inventions made possible the kind of world we know today. Their work was developed in Birmingham because for generations skilled craftsmen have lived there, men capable of working ingeniously and accurately with metal. The whole world is in their debt.

At the end of the twentieth century the British Empire is viewed in a very different light from that in which it was viewed a few decades ago. However, its more beneficial effects include the spread of Britain's industrial knowledge, which in many lands is still relied upon. Roads, railways, buildings, machinery and even whole cities still stand as evidence. Perhaps even more noticeable is the use of the English language, and the availability of literature in that tongue. The speedier, safer communications of the Empire also enabled British missionaries to spread the Christian faith, just as St Paul took advantage of those of the Roman Empire. William Carey, David Livingstone, and Hudson Taylor were among hundreds of dedicated men and women whose sacrifice and acts of faith enlarged the Christian church to which millions in every continent belong.

Great changes have taken place in our world since World War II, not least with respect to mission. There has been a decline in traditional British foreign missionary enterprise following the demise of the Empire. But there has been an upsurge of activity using modern means of communication. This has come not only from the British Isles, or from America, but from an ever growing body of workers from what is now known as the Third World.

The decline referred to was not only for political and economic reasons. Basically it was due to the spiritual decline and lack of effectiveness in the church in Britain. One of the main motivations for starting new city missions and reviving the older ones at home is to rectify this lack. There is a great need and opportunity for in-depth evangelism in the great centres of population. All kinds of valuable experience can be gained in our modern, multi-racial, multicultural cities. Missionary candidates can benefit greatly from time spent serving with city missions. Such courses can also provide an important resource for recruitment of candidates for the mission field.

Steve Jacobs, a senior missionary who had served in India, understood this. In 1967 he referred Peter Skinner to us. He was a young man who had completed Bible College basic training but still felt ill-equipped for the task overseas. Peter spent a year with us at the Birmingham City Mission. He worked with a local church and also helped in the city centre. His experience caused him to develop his skills and grow spiritually.

Soon others were asking to come. By 1972 it was decided that a structured course be introduced and advertised. At the time of writing (1990) 170 young people have spent at least a year on this Inservice Training Course. At first they were accommodated in the homes of well-wishers. Later two houses were acquired for their use. They served individually in local churches but also formed a team for evangelism. Practical training was given on the job by experienced workers, and one day each week was given to study with various clergy and pastors or tutors. No fees were charged; the students were taught the art of prayer and faith for finance. Together with the mission staff they saw God answer in many wonderful ways.

Lessons in faith

A student was sitting in our first-floor lounge area, where lectures were given, feeling very cold, for although there was a gas fire burning the heat was lost in the open stairway adjoining. Much heat could be conserved if a heavy curtain was used as a room divider. But we had no money for such a luxury. Prayer was made. Two weeks later nothing had been done, but as finances were a little easier we decided to buy the curtain fittings and install them. Another two weeks passed and we sat in the cold admiring the fittings, which were still curtainless. Wondering how we could ever afford to buy the material, I walked across the way into our warehouse 'long room'. Just inside the door was a large parcel. It contained two heavy curtains. As we tried them for size we found that curtain hooks were already sewn on. They were a perfect fit. God was teaching the students that they could trust Him in the smallest practical matters. No one ever owned up to having sent the curtains, or carrying them upstairs and putting the parcel where I could not avoid finding it. To this day I still do not know the details. God does.

Money to pay for their lodgings was given to the students on Mondays, their study day. Some money was usually brought in by staff who had been given it on preaching appointments the previous day. Other money would be in the weekend post. Occasionally people would call at the centre to hand it in, while others would just post it anonymously through the letter-box. One Monday this did not happen. Little came in from any source. The day wore on and I was praying earnestly for God to provide. The students having their lectures were unaware of our predicament. In the afternoon still no more money had arrived so I decided that as I had enough money in my own personal bank account I would have to withdraw it. Various demands upon my time left me with just enough time to get to the bank, but as I arrived the doors were shut. I was too late. Returning to my office I paced the floor while continuing to ask God to provide. A file of papers lay on my desk. For some reason I do not know I ran my finger through the papers. Among them I came across a small box, which I had not noticed before. Lifting it up I could see it contained money—just enough to pay the students.

At our conference some months later I related the story. The students registered their disapproval, saying that I should have told them of the problem at the time and not carried the burden alone. Since then we have made a practice of keeping staff and students aware of the financial situation. In times of need we have spread outstanding bills on the floor and held a prayer meeting around them. God has always answered. The exercise has been an invaluable part of the training process.

World vision

God had His own ways of bringing people to us. Steve was on holiday walking alone along the Cornish cliffs when he came across another lonely hiker and they struck up a friendly conversation. They discovered that they were both Christians. The other man worked as cook in the BCM hostel kitchen. Steve had time to spare. Since graduating from university he had worked on a government contract in Papua New Guinea. He was having a long vacation before taking up another lucrative contract. It was agreed that Steve should come to Birmingham to do some voluntary work for the homeless. A few days after his arrival he came to see me.

He had been invited by our students to help in evangelism.
God had moved his heart as he observed their work and he
asked if he too could join the year course. He did. At the end
he declared his interest in overseas missions. He went off to
Bible College, applied to a missionary society and is now a
missionary in Papua New Guinea, where he had previously
worked for the government.

World vision has been emphasised, therefore, from the
inception of our student course and it has resulted in the
mission inspiring participants to look far afield. Africa,
India, Pakistan, Japan, Europe and South America have
received and benefited from their ministry. Other groups
and city missions have since developed year training programmes. It has been our privilege to give the lead. Yet
there are still features of Birmingham's Inservice Training
Course which remain unique.

When Rupert Abbott applied to join the team no one
could have foreseen the events which would follow. He and
his wife Janet had graduated from Leeds University having
studied agricultural zoology. How this could be used in the
wider city was unclear, to say the least. For a time they had
engaged in social work but now they felt the Lord calling
them to the BCM. Although nervous at first, Rupert
developed into an able communicator on the course. Then
he became a staff member and led the student team for a
year. Gradually his burden for the Muslim population grew,
and eventually Rupert and Janet bought a small terraced
house in the downtown area of Saltley where the population
was 70 per cent Muslim.

In order to communicate with their neighbours the couple
studied the Urdu language. They discovered that most of
their neighbours came from one area of northern Pakistan.
So during the year 1987-1988 the Abbotts, with their two
young children, went to live in Pakistan. At Islamabad airport they were met by their former nextdoor neighbour in
Saltley, a Pakistani, who arranged for their hospitality at first

and made it possible for Rupert to visit many families that had connections with Birmingham. When the Abbotts returned to their Birmingham home and their city mission work, they found this venture had created a vital link with the local community.

6

New Life For All

'CAN YOU ACCOMMODATE a few hundred young people for the weekend?' This unusual request was to be the beginning of a long relationship with Operation Mobilisation. One of their leaders, Peter Conlan, came from Birmingham and had come to the Lord through summer camps with which we had been associated. OM was having its annual international conference in London. Peter was asking if the conferees could come to Birmingham for the weekend to help in our evangelism. It was a tall order and we were given only three weeks' notice!

Somehow we managed. In the event only a hundred came, but we also enlisted the help of a hundred students from Birmingham Bible Institute and a hundred of our own volunteers and supporters.

The Central Hall was booked for a Saturday morning training session and an evening meeting addressed by George Verwer, OM's founder and director. During the afternoon the conferees were divided into three groups, one for street witnessing in the city centre, another for visitation in an Asian area and the third for outreach on one of the new suburban housing estates. They were later to return to the centre for a march of witness.

The BCM had the overall responsibility for co-ordinating evangelism, arranging transport, catering, overnight accommodation and relations with the local churches where they would stay and minister on Sunday. But one thing we overlooked in our planning was Sunday lunch. We had arranged for coaches to pick up folk in Bromsgrove Street for their return to London. However, our centre was just not capable of feeding a hundred hungry young people before their journey. The problem only came to light after they had left to sleep overnight in the churches. Next morning I decided to try to save the situation by making discreet phone calls to church secretaries. After giving travel instructions to be relayed to the teams, I mentioned that church members could keep the OMers for lunch if they wished. In the event only eight people came to the centre for lunch!

A similar exercise took place the following year, in 1970. Again we had little notice, but at least we remembered to arrange a Sunday lunch! We were gaining experience. We also had a set of excellent photographs of the OM evangelistic weekend, for the following reason.

Put in the picture

On the Tuesday following OM's first visit, the BCM was holding its usual open-air meeting in the Bull Ring. A young man with camera at the ready and photographic equipment hanging from his shoulder was listening intently. An appeal was made for interested people to come forward for counselling. He came. As is our custom I enquired into his spiritual history. Had he heard the message we were preaching before? He told us that on the previous Saturday he had been following his photographic hobby, taking pictures of people and places in the city. He had become interested in a crowd of young people holding a meeting in the market place. Their earnestness and postures would make a good picture. But he became even more interested in the things which they were saying. Suddenly the meeting closed. Clearly they had another appointment. The young people were of different nationalities and races, yet they seemed very close to one another, almost like a family. He was fascinated by this and also by the happiness which they seemed to have. Joe decided to follow them.

Several members of the group carried placards bearing Christian slogans and Bible texts, which made them easy to follow. However, when they arrived outside Birmingham Town Hall he was amazed to see them being joined by hundreds of other similar young men and women carrying banners.

The whole group marched along the main street singing hymns and choruses. Shoppers stopped to listen and were given literature. Joe followed until they arrived at the large red brick building which is Birmingham's Central Hall. Everyone went inside. Joe went in too. He had not attended a religious meeting before and sat unobtrusively at the back. What the speaker had to say moved him deeply. It was with sadness that he left for home at the end of the meeting. He had been too shy to speak to anyone, yet he wanted to know more. However, as he waited at the bus stop he was joined by a lady with her small son. The lad spoke to Joe and soon he and his mother were talking about Jesus. Before parting they gave him a Gospel of St John and other Christian literature. This he had read. Now, on this following Tuesday, he was ready to receive Christ.

After he had done so a thought occurred to me. Had he taken any photographs of the march? My brother was to have taken some, but I forgot that when I sent him with a team to an outlying suburb, which meant he missed the march. How amazing it was to me that Joe Osgood had not only been present with his camera but had taken a whole series of superb photographs. The Lord knew I needed a photographer. When he was converted he came, pictures and all!

Ready for action

Early in 1971 we were wondering if later that year we would again be invaded by young folk from Operation Mobilisation. We decided to take the initiative and give them a formal invitation. When this was accepted we started to plan a campaign. Christian leaders were invited to meet in four areas. The idea was that we would reach out to the whole city by means of visitation and special meetings. In some districts the very fact that ministers and elders from different denominations were meeting at all was a cause for thanksgiving. Progress was being made.

Reports had been coming in from Africa and South America of the New Life For All crusades. We decided to give ours the same title. BCM personnel wrote articles for a special edition of the *Challenge* newspaper. One hundred thousand copies were printed for our mission. They were bought and distributed by local churches. Training sessions were held, prayer meetings organised and evangelists invited. A local group of leaders formed a committee in the Handsworth area, a multi-racial district. This group was to continue to function, sponsoring many events over a number of years. The evangelistic meetings were held in Cannon Street Memorial Church on the Soho Road, the busy main street.

Another group met on the eastern side of the city. They arranged meetings in Bethel Temple, Ward End, a church built by local people converted at tent missions held by George Jefferies, founder of the Elim church, in 1936. In post-war years this church had gone into decline, but the New Life For All meetings brought a time of refreshing. The evangelist Don Summers held his meetings there, which later led to a large crusade in the city centre.

One group were based at the Pheasey estate, near King-

standing, a vast council housing area, built in the 1930s.
Again it was good to see leaders from different denominations come together for united effort, and this unity continued for a number of years in other ventures.

Kings Heath Baptist Church was the venue for the mission
held on the south side of the city. A number of churches
joined the crusade, which was led by the OM team.

On the final Saturday we were once again joined by a
hundred or so people from the OM conference in London,
and by students from the Birmingham Bible Institute. This
time, however, we had been able to motivate the churches so
that when we held a march of witness over a thousand people
joined in. This was the first major march of its kind to be
held in Birmingham. It was held on Saturday afternoon,
which was prime shopping time, and the march was therefore observed by thousands of people.

Among the shoppers was a family related to a member of
the BCM committee. For many years she had prayed for her
family. Impressed by what they saw and heard, they decided
to go to the evening meeting which was being announced. At
Carrs Lane Church centre they heard the Revd Alan Stevens
speak, and at the end of the meeting the mother responded
to the appeal. During the following winter her three daugh-
ters also became Christians, and the next spring, at another
event organised by the BCM, the father also turned to
Christ. This family went on to be a very effective Christian
unit in a local church, as well as helping in the mission in
many ways.

7

An International Conference

1972 WAS A CRUCIAL YEAR, not only for the mission, but for me personally. Up to this time, despite all the work we accomplished, we had no one full time in the office, and in other departments workers were few, young and inexperienced. The BCM had started in my home at Kingshurst,after I had moved there from Essex in 1961 in order to plant a church on that new housing estate. Within a few years the Chelmsley Wood estate had been built around us, providing homes for 70,000 people. The church was growing and so were the opportunities and responsibilities.

Most of my financial support came from teaching. Since arriving at Kingshurst I had been responsible for teaching several hundred boys religious education. It had been a worthwhile experience, and several of the boys became missionaries, pastors and elders. Now the school had been turned into a mixed comprehensive school for 1,200 children. Although I had cut down my hours of work for several years, it was becoming too much for me. Teaching was becoming more demanding. I was leading and planting a new church, and we were at the stage of putting up a new building. And I was leading the fast growing Birmingham City Mission. That is not to mention that I had a wife and four rapidly growing children! Something had to change. I decided to give up teaching in July.

The timing may have been connected with the OM conference. We had already been involved in several special conference weekends. While making the arrangements I had visited the conference bases in London. Previously they had used a jam factory in Catford—a huge draughty building which somehow served the purpose, but not too well. I had had the temerity to suggest that this year they held the conference in Birmingham and that the BCM would find a venue.

Operation Mobilisation is an international training organisation, which began in Mexico in 1957. Thousands of young people, and some not so young, have passed through the programme. Most people spend a month or so in the summer, first in conference, and then working in teams engaging chiefly in literature evangelism. Areas reached are mainly countries and districts where there are few evangelical Christian churches. The recruits come from many different countries and speak different languages, so the teams are international. Training is given in discipleship, community living and various forms of communicating the gospel. The emphasis is on Bible study, prayer, holy living and a simple lifestyle. From the beginning, teams are taught to depend upon God to supply their needs. They are also made aware of the spiritual needs of countries throughout the world, and there is a great deal of travelling.

At the end of the summer the international conference is held for those who wish to apply to stay longer than a few weeks. Some remain for a year or two. An increasing number are long-termers. Speakers of high spiritual quality address the main meetings. Country leaders select people suitable for their own lands. Specialised training is given to particular groups, such as drivers and secretaries. At the same time passports and visas are sorted out and medical preparation is made. From the conference people move out throughout Europe and Asia. At the time to which we are referring, OM had recently acquired a missionary ship, the *Logos*, which left for India.

It seemed easy enough. All we had to do was find a vacant building large enough to accommodate 600 people, an auditorium for a thousand, rooms for discussion and prayer groups, offices, dining room and kitchen! And we wanted it for nothing. At first we looked at a large department store in the city centre. On reflection it would not have been suitable, but we were refused anyway. Then we began weighty correspondence with various companies who had factories and offices for sale and to let. We merely wanted to borrow one for six weeks. Back came the replies, no, no, no! The city council was approached, and they suggested the disused BBC broadcasting centre in Broad Street. So I made an appointment to meet an official there. It was hard to park the car near the centre, and I had to drive around for a while until I found a parking meter. As I stopped I noticed a large disused warehouse and office block. No signs indicated who the owner was or where he could be contacted. I kept my appointment, but having inspected the broadcasting centre decided it was not suitable.

Many weeks of searching and waiting followed. All kinds of leads were followed up but to no avail. At the beginning of August there was still no news. I had to leave the situation as my church was having a holiday houseparty on the Scottish border, and I was responsible. People were having a good time, but I was not enjoying it. In a few weeks hundreds of people were due to arrive in Birmingham for a conference which the mission had agreed to convene, but still we had no place to hold it. Eventually I could stand it no longer. One afternoon, after we had just come back from the beach, I discussed my burden with the other church leaders. It was agreed that I should leave the organisation of the holiday with them and return to my duties in the city.

The promise of premises

The following morning, after driving most of the night, I looked at our options. One possibility was a little used, but large church on the east side. I collected a small group of leaders to consider the matter. It would be difficult as we would need additional premises some distance away. Among the leaders was Norman Evans, who had helped us with the rating problem of Bromsgrove Street and had asked if he could be of assistance. Suddenly I remembered the warehouse I had seen when I parked on my visit to the broadcasting centre. I told him about it and asked if he would make it his business to find the owner and enquire about its use. Later in the afternoon I was in my office when the phone rang. It was Norman. He had located the person responsible for the premises and spoken to him. I rang this man in London and explained what we were looking for and why. He was interested and asked me to put our request in writing. At once I drove round to the typist who was helping me at the time. She typed the letter, I posted it and then drove back to Scotland. A few days later when I returned from the holiday a letter awaited me telling me we could have the full use of the Parker Winder & Achurch building—free. We collected the keys.

Broad Street is one of the major thoroughfares on the west side of the city, on which lie the impressive Baskerville House, built of white stone, and the domed Hall of Memory. On its north side lovely gardens front the attractive modern Repertory Theatre. These, and other stately buildings nearby made the place where the conference was to be held an ideal location.

The PWA building was constructed in the 1930s as a showroom, office block and warehouse. No one thought it would become a meeting place for a thousand people from more than twenty countries. To create an auditorium it was necessary to remove centre walls. A kitchen and dining area had to be improvised. Fortunately all the lights and electrically operated lifts were in working order. But it was bereft of furniture.

The first thing to do was to get the place clean. A young married American girl arrived with her husband, who was a mechanic. He could turn his hand to fix almost anything. But his wife seemed to disappear. Eventually I found her. For three days she had been cleaning walls, including those of the stairways.

The large retail area and showroom had been used to display bathrooms and kitchens suitable for the homes of millionaires. The floor was highly polished and needed little attention. We considered how we could make the best use of it. Why not hold a missionary exhibition? But where could we get the exhibits at such short notice?

A few phone calls revealed that the Christian Holiday Conference at Filey was due to end just as ours was due to start. Many missionary societies had personnel and exhibits there and they were willing and able to transport everything direct from Filey to Birmingham.

On the Broad Street front of the building were huge display windows. Making an attractive display would be a major task. Among the OM vanguard we discovered two German artists, who agreed to be responsible for window-dressing. When I arrived the following morning I was amazed to find the work completed. They had worked all day and night to finish it.

Klaus was a German engineer, who was responsible for creating an auditorium out of the warehouse. I have never met a more practical or hard-working man. His emergency plumbing and carpentry soon also created a large kitchen complete with sinks and cookers.

Suddenly we were confronted with a serious problem. Our efforts had been observed by the fire officer, whose offices were right opposite our building. He came in to see what was going on and promptly announced that we could not hold a conference there. The building was not intended

to hold so many people. I explained to him that we had no
option. Hundreds of people were already on their way from
distant lands to this address. Then I asked what needed to be
done to use the building for the purpose planned. He gave
me a list. Most alterations we could do easily, but one was
difficult. A large fire exit was required at the rear of the
auditorium. Unfortunately the building was on the side of a
hill. The entrance was level with the street but at the rear the
floor was more than twenty feet from the ground. An exit
would need ramps and they would have to be strong and
wide enough to carry 200 people at a time. Handrails and
artificial light were also required.

Klaus set to work. First he had to knock a hole in the wall
about twelve feet wide. Then he needed to construct sliding
doors. After two days he called me to see the results. It was
incredible. All was in order, including the ramps. But where
had he got all the materials from? He took me down the
ramps and across a yard to a large old factory. The keys
given to us included ones which gave us access to this.
Because the place was so old, dirty, and full of junk we had
decided not to use it. When Klaus opened the door I could
hardly believe my eyes. Previously it had been a two-storey
building. Now it had only one! The place was clean and in it
were a number of OM Volkswagen vans. It had become the
mechanic's base and indoor carpark. As I looked up at the
new high ceiling he explained that he had sawn the upper
floor from its joists and used it for the ramps for the fire exit.

At first the fire officer was still not satisfied, but I called
our solicitor and he came with the city architect. They were
so astonished and pleased with what they saw that they
instructed the officer to leave us alone to get on 'with the
admirable conference'. Turning to Klaus, the architect said,
'This work must have cost thousands of pounds, how much
did you pay?' 'Oh, I only bought a bag of nails,' was his
matter-of-fact reply.

Because the conferees were from so many different

nations it was necessary to arrange for translation facilities. A soundproof area was made for the translators, so they could hear the message on earphones and translate over the microphones to the twelve different language groups. The arrangements were highly professional and successful.

Soon the conferees began to arrive. I was concerned about food supplies. The caterer had not yet been seen and meals would need to be served. Organising the first food purchase became a matter of urgency. Later I was introduced to Jeanie Sales, the capable cook. As I showed her round Birmingham wholesale market I told her of my concern about her late arrival. To my amazement she explained that she had been delayed on the journey. She had been spending the summer evangelising in Israel and had just driven a truck overland via Syria, Turkey, Yugoslavia and other European countries. No wonder she was late.

Some arrivals had been extremely resourceful. One day, when I was at our Bromsgrove Street shop, I noticed a young man peering at the Bible which was open in the window. When I asked if I could help him he showed me a piece of paper which simply bore the words 'Operation Mobilisation, Birmingham'. He told me he had just arrived and wanted to find these people. Leaving the coach station he had just wandered along the streets until he noticed the Bible. Of course I was able to take him to the conference. It was quite obvious that he came from distant parts. When asked from where, he replied, 'Khartoum'. He had travelled all the way from the Sudan to us with just that scrap of paper showing his destination.

It was a good thing that at the rear of the PWA building there were vehicle loading bays because soon goods began to arrive. Chairs, tables, desks and furniture of all kinds were given or loaned by churches and private individuals. Gifts of clothing also came. This was the supply for 'Charlie', the stock from which OM personnel could be fitted out themselves. They had no money for new clothes. Clothing des-

tined for people in need in the Third World was also part of
the cargo of the ship *Logos*, sailing east.

When the conference got under way we felt that the
BCM's part was finished. We had seen God answer prayer in
giving us the venue. And accommodation had been provided
for 600 people in churches in fellowship with the mission.
Through our contacts we had also been able to supply specialist personnel such as doctors and nurses, together with
the necessary medical supplies. Then we had publicised the
event so that the Christian public attended the main meetings, necessitating the use of an overflow room with close-
circuit television. Finally we had arranged Saturday evangelism, culminating in a march of witness around the city streets
led by an open-topped, double-decker London bus, which
had been used for outreach at the Munich Olympics. This
march ended in Victoria Square outside the Town Hall.
Hundreds of people listened to the preaching, which finished
with a call for prayer. That spectacle of so many people
kneeling in prayer in the city's main square will always live in
my memory.

8

Kingshurst—Where It All Began

'GREAT OAKS FROM LITTLE ACORNS GROW.' The thought occurred to us as we stood beneath an oak tree, waiting for a bus one summer evening. Stanley Walker, who was with me, frequently referred to it in succeeding years, even making a visual aid using the idea to depict the growth of the mission. Stan and Doreen had moved from Essex to Birmingham in 1961 to work as children's evangelists in Nechells. We had known each other in Bible College days and it had seemed natural to me to invite him to be a member of the new city mission committee, where he faithfully served until called to higher service in heaven in 1986.

The seed of the BCM oak first began to grow in Kingshurst, in 1965, and this record would be incomplete without some reference to the events which took place there.

Being called of God is an awesome business, and my wife and I had no doubt that we were being called. For some years we had been involved in church planting in London County Council estates in Essex. Three fellowships were formed, and one church building constructed, which is being well used today. Our home had been leased to us for evan-

gelism and that lease was ending. We felt no liberty to apply
for a renewal but rather drawn to return to our city of origin.
On two occasions different people had mentioned Kingshurst as a place to live and work. We applied to both
Birmingham and Meriden councils for housing on the same
terms as those in Essex. Both refused, but on the morning
we heard we received a visitor, Mrs Emblen, whom we had
not seen for several months. She had received money from
property which had been bought from her by the government. While praying she felt that God told her clearly to
offer it to us as a private low interest mortgage to buy a
house in Birmingham. Thus the Lord met our need.

As we were taking young people away to camp during the
month of August we packed up all our household belongings, believing God would give us a house at Kingshurst.
Dorothy and the children never returned! Taking a day off
from camp at Malvern we visited Kingshurst but could find
no house for sale. We went into the city and placed an advert
for a house in the *Birmingham Evening Mail*. I prayed that
the first reply would be for the house God wanted us to live
in. Some days later I learned that my brother John, whose
address we put in the advert, had had one reply only, but
thought the house in question was too big and too expensive
for us. However, I immediately went to see it. It was ideal,
but required more money than we possessed. I told the
owner, who was not a Christian, why we wanted to live in
Kingshurst, and that if he wanted to contact me again I
would be visiting my brother in a week's time. As it was a
sellers' market, and he showed me several letters applying
for his house, it did not seem likely, but the next week he
called to see me.

'Please come back and look at my house again,' he
pleaded. We went there, and sitting down together he told
us, 'I want you to have this house. Since meeting you I
have felt unable to reply to the other applicants. I have not

been able to sleep for thinking of you and the work you want to do. You must have this house.'

'You know I haven't enough money,' I said.

He replied, 'I will bring the price down and can arrange the remainder as I am an insurance broker. Have you got £5?'

I happened to have it so I gave it to him.

'That will pay for the fire insurance. We will call it a deal, the house is yours,' he declared.

This semi-detached house on a large corner site with a private drive and garage became the birthplace of both the Kingshurst Evangelical Church and the Birmingham City Mission.

First we held a Sunday school for our own children and those of our neighbours. Peter Wright, a child who lived next door, is today a fine Christian married to a Christian lady he met at a camp associated with the BCM. Several other neighbours and their children were also brought to Christ and serve Him now.

On the first Wednesday in the house we held a prayer meeting. A small number gathered and we prayed for more. Especial mention was made of a block of flats which had just been built, and we asked that a Christian family might move in. The next week our fourth baby arrived and I visited Dorothy in hospital. Returning home I found the prayer meeting in progress and joined in, praying again that God would send Christians into the new block of flats. I felt a piece of paper being pushed into my hand. On it was written 'God has answered that prayer!' There followed the name and address of Mr and Mrs Saunders. To this day they are faithful supporters of the BCM.

The group meeting in our home consisted, besides ourselves, of my brother John, who also became a founder member of the BCM, his wife Jean, David Torpey, who later became full-time administrator of the BCM, his wife Phyllis, and Mrs Lily Moulden. They were soon joined by John and

Muriel Wager, whose eldest daughter, Pauline, was the first
to be baptised and later became a Worldwide Evangelisation
Crusade missionary to Chad. Pamela Collins, a young Faith
Mission worker, also joined, and she too became a founder
member of the BCM. Her prayerful, radiant Christian life
added much to the mission until her death following a long
illness.

New home—new job

In order to pay expenses I needed a job. For five years I had
worked as part-time head of Religious Education in an Essex
secondary school. I sought a similar post in Birmingham, but
to no avail. Remembering that Kingshurst was in Warwickshire, I wrote for an advertised Warwickshire post at
Kingsbury, about eight miles away. The job had been taken
but, to my surprise, I received application forms with a letter
asking me to complete them. If I did so they would try to find
me a job. Then I was astonished to be asked to go to
Kingshurst High School for Boys for an interview by the
headmaster. He was an irreligious man who said he had no
vacancies and wondered why I had been sent to him. As we
talked we discovered that I had been converted by the outreach of a church which he used to attend, and had been
baptised by his father! He found me a job and soon I was
head of RE. I remained there for eleven years.

After my first lesson I asked the boys who did not belong
to any youth organisation to attend a meeting in a home to
form a Covenanter group. Twenty-four non-Christian boys
turned up, including Ray Wootton. He has continued ever
since and is now an elder in the church. John Pennell,
mentioned later, also joined soon after and went on to be a
missionary in France. Then came Derek Purnell, who is now
a pastor in Manchester, and Wesley Erpen, now BCM field
leader. Owen Nicholds became another church elder, his
brother Billy serving the Lord in Lancashire. Peter Lea is a
deacon and David Moulden a missionary in Pakistan.

Not to be outdone, Dorothy, my wife, gave out leaflets at the girls' school inviting them to start a Girl Covenanter group. Jackie Brown later married Wesley Erpen, went to Bible College and now serves as a pastor's wife. Maureen Judd married Derek Purnell and has a similar role. Others came, were converted and added to the church. Now their children are part of the growing community. Prayer was made that a Christian teacher should come on to the girls' school staff. Soon the prayer was answered. Pauline Lineham arrived and was a great help to the Christian girls. One pupil invited her home because her elder sister was interested in the Bible. This led to the conversion of Erika James, who joined the church and became a missionary to Chad.

Outgrown!

Initially all the services were held in our home in Wheeley Moor Road. Soon we could no longer get all the children in but were able to hire a local tenants' hall on Sunday afternoons. When the Covenanter groups were too large for the house they also moved, followed by the family morning service. Eventually the Sunday school outgrew the tenants' hall so it was moved to a junior school. Evening services were started there monthly, and finally weekly.

People asked to be baptised or married, and we therefore had to borrow church buildings in other districts. Within weeks of arriving at Kingshurst we had applied to the council for a plot of land on which to build a church. We were refused on the grounds that all available land was already allocated and that adjoining farm land was 'green belt' and could not be built upon. A few years later we heard that a vast housing estate was to be built on that land. An application was immediately made again and this time we secured a prime site in Cooks Lane.

Being on a busy main road the new church site could not be missed. To its rear several residential tower blocks were built and also many houses. The problem of the site was that it was very low-lying land, just a hole waiting to be filled in. In the spring of 1971 a service of dedication led by Dr David Rigby, principal of Lebanon Missionary Bible College, was held around the hole. Later it cost several thousand pounds to fill the hole and build foundations. Then we ran out of money. While we were raising funds for the next stage the young church decided to hire a large marquee and hold a tent mission on the concrete platform.

The Jesus tent

'Have you been to the Jesus tent yet?' asked the little boy, blocking the pavement with his bicycle.

'What do you mean?' asked the lady, whose interest was aroused at once.

'There's a tent in the field and they tell you all about Jesus,' he replied.

Ruth Wragg decided there and then that she would go and hear for herself. Her son Jeffery had attended the school where I taught. He had gone on to be a teacher himself and then emigrated to Australia. But his marriage had broken down. Ruth was desperate to help her only son but distance made it impossible. She began to pray for him, but felt guilty, being aware that she knew nothing of God, had never attended church and didn't even know where to start. The little boy's question pointed her to the tent mission being held with the help of the BCM while the Kingshurst church was being built. Ruth became a Christian and served as a bookkeeper in the BCM hostel before joining her son in Australia. Now all the family are Christians in active service for the Lord.

Phil Smith and his mother stood looking at the notice-board beside the tent. As they did so they were invited in. After his conversion Phil and his wife and family sold their home, went to Bible College and Phil became a pastor.

A building for God's people

Thus the church grew. So did its relationship with the city mission. Some were converted through the work of the BCM, others helped the BCM in its work. For my part it would have been difficult to carry the responsibilities of founding a mission without a strong, praying and supportive church in the background.

The church existed for a number of years without a building of its own. When the new building opened in 1976 it was immediately filled and became the focal point for evangelising a wide area of East Birmingham. The city mission's Christian Telephone Service transferred its equipment there, and it also became a base for outreach to the new National Exhibition Centre nearby.

'God loved me as I was'

On a bright September morning the fresh intake of eleven-year-old schoolboys lined up nervously in their new uniforms to be inspected by the headmaster. As the roll-call rang out, the lad who responded to the name 'John Pennell' made an instant impression. He was the smallest boy there, wearing the regulation black blazer and grey shorts, but had a crew-cut hairstyle, a round face and an impish grin.

John was soon to join the Kingshurst Covenanters, and as the years went on he became a firm Christian. When he left school he worked in a local butcher's shop, where he became known for his Christian witness. In the summer of 1972 he went to France with Operation Mobilisation, just for a month, we thought. That was not to be, for eighteen years later he is still there serving the Lord. He married a French girl, Elise, and they have three lovely children. Besides being involved in church planting he has had wide responsibilities in publishing and distributing Christian literature in French.

There was one interlude. Shortly after their marriage the

Pennells spent a year in England, on the BCM Inservice Training Course, with John as team leader.

The mission held a tent campaign on the Stechford fairground in 1976. There John's mother committed her life to Christ and became a bright, shining witness at home, at work and as a member of the new church at Kingshurst. She became an outstanding prayer warrior and supporter of the BCM. In 1987 she and Mrs Moulden travelled to Pakistan to visit missionaries. On her return she developed a crippling disease which a few months later led to her death. During her final days she was an inspiration to all and the means of conversion of another lady who is now in the church.

The relationship between Kingshurst and BCM was further strengthened when in 1982 Jeremy Andrews was appointed city missionary to the district. He and his wife Rosalind bought a home there and were successful in bringing several people to Christ. Jean Roberts was one and this is her testimony.

> For fifty years I thought that by being born in England and living a reasonably decent life I was a Christian. The Bible was a stranger to me.
>
> One day Jeremy Andrews and his friend Ian knocked on my door. They were working for the Birmingham City Mission and doing their door-to-door work around Kingshurst that week. Jeremy asked if I believed that Jesus Christ had died for me on the cross. I wasn't very responsive. In fact I was rather rude. 'I'm not sure there is a God,' I said. 'If there is, why are all these bad things happening in the world?' As I said, I was not very responsive. Jeremy left a tract with me and I promptly forgot about them. But the Lord hadn't forgotten me. Three times that week I was challenged in odd ways by the question, 'Jesus died on the cross for me, so what am I going to do about it?'
>
> The address on the tract led me to Kingshurst Evangelical Church which is attended by quite a few people who work for BCM, including Jeremy and Ian.
>
> There I found Jesus. I thought I had to cleanse my life

'EVERY PICTURE TELLS A STORY'

Bull Ring Centre and Rotunda building

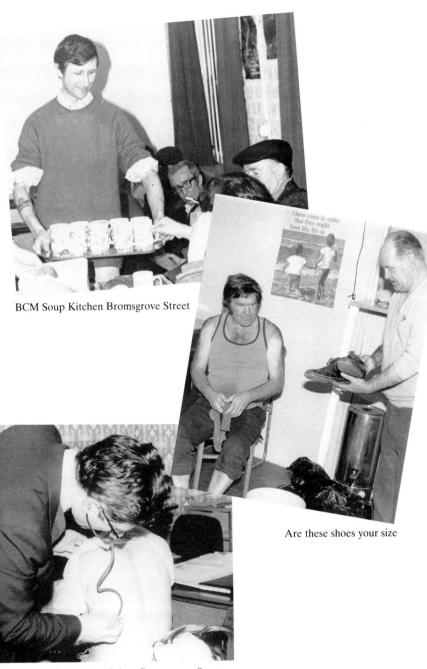

BCM Soup Kitchen Bromsgrove Street

Are these shoes your size

Dr Aylin's clinic at Bromsgrove Street

Wesley Erpen preaching in the Bull Ring

Hospital visitation

Preparing the toys at Christmas

Visiting a one parent family

'Message' the Christian Telephone Service

Christmas bookselling

A place of our own

Children's open air mission

Exhibition evangelism

Tent Mission

Kingshurt Evangelical Church

Visiting the elderly

Visitation in Winson Green

Hostel for the homeless

Lower wing of the hostel

BCM Charity Shop

'Day Death Died' Exhibition

Street witnessing in Birmingham

In the Bull Ring 1969

In the Bull Ring 1990

Exhibition in Bull Ring Centre Court

The hostel being re-built

Feeding the homeless

Celebrating our 21st birthday

The re-opening of BCM Hostel

Making good use of the Odeon Cinema

Supporting Mission England 1984

The Arden Road Centre

Visiting at Quinton

Students study day

The General Office

BCM Finance Office

Praying in Victoria Square 1972

Margaret Anderson at No. 36

The 'New Life For All' Campaign 1971

Preaching from the top of a bus 1972

BCM choir and orchestra

Audience at the BCM Silver Jubilee Concert

The BCM Care Bus in action

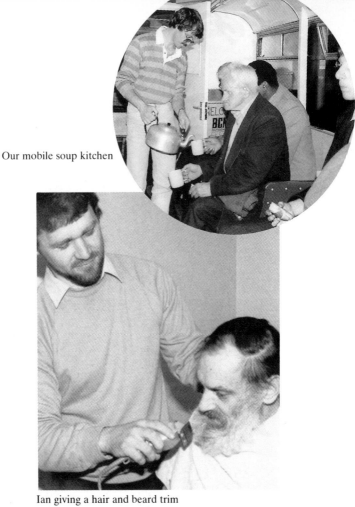

Our mobile soup kitchen

Ian giving a hair and beard trim

Ian Hare
at work

before inviting Jesus into my heart. How wrong can one be? Jesus Himself showed me in His own special way that He loved me as I was, with all my faults; that He was hurt because I was holding back, and that He was alive in a real, vital way. My life has so changed and been enriched since asking Him into my heart that I am amazed that I never realised how wonderful knowing Jesus could be.

The young people from the BCM must have to deal with hundreds of people whose reaction was like mine was. But there are many, too, who must be grateful as I am for their perseverance in their service to the Lord through the BCM.

Other people who came to the Lord as a result of Jeremy's visitation included Dennis and Mary Vernon. They have given wonderful practical help to the church, and their daughter Helen later married my son Ian, now in full-time Christian service.

9

Planting A Church At Castle Vale

'**C**OULD YOU TELL ME how long the mission will go on?'

The caller was a young clergyman who had received information about the BCM through the post. Apparently he thought that a city mission was an event which would be over in a few days or weeks. This is a common misconception. In fact we hope that the city mission will function as long as it is required. It is viewed by us as a kind of police force, not to keep law and order but rather to rescue those who have broken God's law, and make them into new, law-abiding people.

A gospel rescue mission has been defined as:

> An arm of the church given to a soul-saving ministry among rejected and neglected peoples everywhere. A home mission station where Christianity is practised every day out of every year. It is a gospel-orientated agency dedicated to helping those people the church does not reach. Although it may be called upon to aid an individual's domestic or material need, this is over-shadowed by the paramount task of preaching the gospel of our Lord Jesus Christ to all who will hear. Yes, the gospel rescue mission strives to set people on their feet, but

more important, it strives to start them walking with God (International Union of Gospel Missions).

The result of such work is to build up the churches. The 1875 report of the Birmingham Town Mission stated that after all their work they could not point to the results, as these had been passed on to local churches. The city mission is therefore not a threat or rival to the church. Some would describe it as a para-church movement, and this is true in a sense, but not wholly so because all its members belong to local churches and it exists to support the church. However, there are districts where no local church exists and where new converts cannot be referred. Such was the case at Castle Vale, a large estate built in the late sixties to house 20,000 people.

The area was once an airfield. During World War II planes were made in the Nuffield factory opposite and then tested and flown out from Castle Bromwich. The post-war British Industries Fair was held on this site, attended by thousands of industrialists from overseas. Because of the great shortage of homes at that time it was decided to build a housing estate there, composed mainly of high-rise flats. These tower blocks were named after aircraft, and the streets after famous airfields.

Much prayer was made for this small town before the people arrived. A Christian lady told how her father used to visit the homes of the airmen with the gospel. When I heard that building had began I felt a burden to walk the freshly laid roads praying for the people who would come. In 1966 our first volunteer team visited the newly occupied homes— 200 in all—presenting each with a copy of the Scriptures. The following year more than forty helpers visited the growing estate, holding open-air meetings for children and adults and talking to people on their doorsteps. Names and addresses of people who were interested in the message were recorded to be followed up.

One particular Saturday morning stands out in my memory. I had no car, so to reach Castle Vale I took the bus to the nearest point, which was about a mile from the tower blocks. It was raining and cold but as I walked I felt an inward glow of expectation as I prayed that that day a Christian home would be found in which meetings could take place. The first visits were fruitless as the people were out. Finally I reached the fourteenth floor of a block of flats. An elderly lady opened the door and as soon as I said who I was she cried, 'Oh, please come in, we've been looking forward to someone visiting us. We wanted to offer our home as a meeting place if you would like to use it.' Mr Carter, her husband, was a disabled man, unable to work, and therefore they were poor, but they really loved the Lord and were willing to give what they had to Him. With the use of this home we were able to commence Bible study meetings, and each Thursday for two years I went regularly, gathering together the first group of believers on the estate.

'Come to our new Sunday school'

Thousands of people were on Birmingham's housing lists, waiting for a new home. Many had married as soon as the war was over and been compelled by the scarcity of property to live with parents or crowd into decaying buildings. To work out priorities of need the council operated a points system. The more children you had, the more points were awarded, and so you moved to the top of the list. Castle Vale therefore teemed with children. This constituted a real challenge to the new church. But how could they reach the children without a suitable building?

The answer soon came. Birmingham City Council decided to build a tenants' hall, a place for all kinds of community activities. I received an invitation to the opening ceremony and was amazed at the off-hand way this beautifully furnished and equipped building was handed over to residents, without any apparent check being made on their character, ability or experience. Needless to say, there were difficult days ahead.

However, Turnhouse Hall proved to be the ideal place to start a Sunday school and later an evening service. In order to bring in the children I typed some notices with my old portable typewriter and duplicated them on a semi-rotary machine. Then, after our own Sunday morning service, I went over to Castle Vale and simply walked around the area within sight of the new hall, handing out the leaflets to children I met. The first afternoon sixty-seven children turned up for the new Sunday school. They were enthusiastic and well behaved. It was the beginning of a work among the boys and girls which still continues.

Looking for leaders

The work of planting a church in a new housing area is a long-drawn-out affair. Part of our problem was that the people came from districts where there was no spiritual life, few churches and little Bible knowledge. Few professional people were in the local community; teachers, doctors and businessmen lived elsewhere. There was a lack of natural leaders. Several mission personnel volunteered to live on the estate, but they were usually young, single men. At last a couple, Gordon and Glenys Sitch, who first met while working for the mission, decided to give all their spare time to the young church. Later they bought a house and enlarged it for meetings. It is now an independent Christian fellowship over which the BCM has no jurisdiction. A full-time BCM missionary, Ian Hare, does live there now with his wife and family, but he is not officially connected with the church. His brief is to continue the work of evangelism by regular visitation and any other means possible.

The best Friend

Each home on the estate has been visited by our mission team several times, and much literature has been distributed. We have also held two tent missions.

Erecting a large marquee in such a place is a risky business. Hundreds of teenagers roam the streets looking for excitement. The tent mission was fair game. On one occasion we heard that a mob of young people drinking in a local pub were planning to come late that night to demolish the tent. We remained in the tent praying for the Lord to help us. At midnight they arrived, a strong crowd of coarse, aggressive youngsters. As they approached we stood near the tent door. Their leader came towards me until he stood within arm's length of the tent. To our astonishment he paused, swayed and fell headlong on the ground. He was the worse for drink but had got as far as the tent and then collapsed unconscious. His friends were so amazed and afraid that they simply picked him up and carried him away. We saw nothing of that group again.

As the estate abounded with children, most of whom had never been inside a church or Sunday school, we held a number of children's missions on the green spaces which served as recreation grounds between the tower blocks. We went to where the children were already playing, put up our board and easel and started playing music on a concertina. Within a few moments we would be surrounded by children. Producing some attractive Bible text cards, we offered them to children who could bring others within five minutes. When this had been done we repeated the process, offering a Scripture booklet. Using this method of good-natured bribery we could assemble a hundred children within fifteen minutes. They were then taught bright choruses and a text to memorise. Finally they heard the wonderful stories of Jesus.

During our second tent mission in Farnborough Road, Castle Vale, we discovered that the canvas had been cut with a knife. The local children were quick to point out the culprit. He was a wild little lad who gave us verbal abuse from the distance to which he had fled.

'It's all right, I'm not going to hurt you,' I called, refusing to chase him. 'I just want to talk to you and explain what the tent is for.'

At first he refused to come, but stayed hovering around until his pals brought him to me, assuring him I wasn't angry.

'This tent is for your use,' I said. 'You can come in any time. We want you to have a good time and we also want to help you and tell you about the best Friend you can have.'

I talked for a while about Jesus and he listened carefully. Suddenly he cried, 'Can I mend the tent? I haven't got any money to pay for it to be done, but I can bring a needle and cotton and sew it up!'

I explained that I didn't think that would work, but if he was sorry for what he had done he could show it by coming to the meetings. He came into the tent then, and attended each meeting for the rest of the week. On the last night an appeal was made. To my joy I noticed that little boy go forward first and I decided to counsel him myself. I showed him the story of Zacchaeus in Luke's Gospel and how Jesus knew all about him, called him to Himself and changed the selfish tax collector into a kind and generous man. Then I read him the verse, 'The Son of Man has come to seek and to save that which was lost.' 'Have you ever heard these words before?' I asked.

'Yes,' he answered, to my surprise. 'When I was small some people came to the green near where I live and they told us about Jesus. They sang some songs and taught me those words. Each night when I go to bed I say this to myself, "The Son of Man has come to seek and to save that which was lost."'

Here was fruit indeed from our children's mission mentioned earlier.

Fruit in due season

Despite all our efforts in Castle Vale not many people
became Christians in our early years of evangelism. God,
however, works in His own wonderful ways. One of our
voluntary workers who faithfully visited the estate prayed
very much for people to come to the Lord. He saw no fruit of
his own, but a member of his church in Selly Oak did. She
was a patient in hospital and in the next bed was a lady in
great need. Through her witness the Christian was able to
lead this lady, Mrs Coaton, to Christ. As she came from
Castle Vale she was introduced to our voluntary worker,
who was able to encourage her and put her in touch with the
newly formed Christian Fellowship. She became a stalwart
Christian, and opened up her home for regular ladies' meetings. She also offered accommodation for Andrew Boyle, a
young BCM worker who gave up his job as a civil engineer to
work for the Lord in the area.

Since 1985 Ian Hare has systematically visited homes on
the estate. His diligence has resulted in quite a number of
people committing their lives to Christ and joining the local
Castle Vale Christian Fellowship.

10

Exhibition Evangelism

THE OPENING of the National Exhibition Centre was a grand affair and the city of Birmingham was proud to own the centre. It lies close to the motorway network and is served by the specially constructed Birmingham International railway station, with fast trains to London and the North, and by the new international airport, with flights worldwide. The airport is connected to the NEC by a unique monorail system. Almost the whole population of the city visited the halls during the first exhibition. Admission was free. It seemed clear to us that here was an evangelistic opportunity that was not to be missed. The following year the BCM took a big step of faith.

Some months earlier David Jebson, superintendent of the Liverpool City Mission, had shared with us his experiences of building a grotto with working models on a Bible theme. He now agreed to loan us some equipment and to visit Birmingham to help set up a display at the International Ideal Home Exhibition at the NEC. Plans were drawn up and submitted to the authorities. The space alone for the seventeen-day show would cost £3,000. Then we had to pay for all the materials and publicity. But it was worth it.

First we had to find a workforce of Christian volunteers with special skills. In addition to Mr and Mrs Jebson and their daughter, who worked so hard on the working models, we needed carpenters, painters, electricians, shop-fitters and window-dressers. Soon we had constructed eight large display boxes in which colourful working models were placed, controlled by electric motors and fishing lines and illuminated by powerful spotlights. Each box measuring eight feet by four feet contained a scene from the parable of the Rich Fool. They were made and stored at Kingshurst until the appointed day when they were taken by truck to the NEC.

A contractor had been employed to build an exhibition 'shell' which would house a bookshop and display of Tearcraft goods—cottage industry products from poorer countries. Within the stall we placed the Rich Fool scenes, arranging them in a circle. The first scene faced the main thoroughfare and attracted public attention. People then progressed in sequence, viewing each episode of the parable, depicted by the working models, until the final challenge of the story. At this point the area was walled so that as viewers moved around the rest of the Good News Exhibition they had opportunities to be counselled, receive free literature or buy Good News Bibles and other books from the stand.

We estimated that about 100,000 people came to the stand, many buying quantities of Christian books and Tearcraft. The exhibition was manned by mission staff and volunteers from early morning to late evening each day. For us it was an enormous undertaking which we will never forget, and from which we gained invaluable experience. At the conclusion we were all quite exhausted, but full of joy that so many had co-operated in a venture which had reached a multitude with the gospel. We were also thankful that all the bills had been paid.

Centre court publicity

Towards the end of the exhibition we began to feel that, having made so much effort and assembled such a fine display, it would be a pity for it to be destroyed. Surely we could use it elsewhere. One day I went into the city centre looking for any place where it could be used. Above the main railway station is the Birmingham Shopping Centre, a large air-conditioned shopping precinct. Near the fountain in the centre is an exhibition area. Thinking about the possibilities, I made my way to the office, but was given a firm refusal. Excuses were made but it seemed obvious they didn't want anything religious in the mall. I left the offices and walked into the adjoining Bull Ring Shopping Centre where shops and markets on different levels surround a centre court, which is used for large exhibitions. As I looked at this prestigious area I suddenly felt that this could be the venue for our display. However, I could not locate the manager's office so I asked a security man for directions.

'It's hard to find,' he said, 'and he won't be there. He will have gone home by now.'

'Would you show me where it is so that I can call some other time?' I asked.

He led me up the long escalator to the top parade and then along the passageway. In an obscure corner was the office and a man was just locking the door. It was the manager, who had been delayed and was late leaving. I introduced myself as director of the Birmingham City Mission. He immediately replied, 'Oh I am glad to meet you. I saw your exhibition at the NEC and was so impressed that I intended to write to you and ask if you would bring it here and display it in our Bull Ring centre court!'

He reopened his office and opened his diary to find us a suitable date. The vacancy was at the end of October when the schools closed for their half-term holidays, an ideal slot as it is one of the busiest times for family outings to the city.

Remembering we had paid £3,000 for the NEC space I

asked rather tentatively how much this site would cost. 'You are doing an important job and you are a charity,' he answered, 'can you afford £100?'

The exhibition in the Bull Ring centre court was more difficult than at the NEC. Because the site was in a shopping centre the erection of the display had to take place on Sunday and be dismantled on Saturday evening. Also, it was not so easy to find professional contractors available to help. However, we went about it prayerfully and things worked out well. The main difficulty was regarding personnel. We had no full-time secretary and even my part-time secretary was away at this time. A newly appointed staff member also left. But we needed more helpers than before as the area was wide open to the public who had free access from early morning to late in the evening. Far more people would see the exhibition here than before.

As in the NEC, we also planned to sell Tearcraft products. People who are desperately in need can manufacture beautiful articles from local, natural materials. Producing and selling these goods is much better than begging or simply being given money. The Evangelical Alliance Relief Fund founded Tearcraft as a means of marketing these items. We have sold thousands of pounds' worth of Tearcraft goods at our exhibitions and elsewhere. Besides helping people abroad it does bring in a little money, but more importantly it creates an interest among people who appreciate more what we do than what we say.

The centre court is very high. Our problem was how to display the Tearcraft goods and make use of this high space. There seemed to be no solution, so on the Friday before the exhibition I visited the area to get some ideas. I was amazed to see a tall scaffolding tower situated at the centre of the site. A notice on it read, 'You may hire this tower for £7 a week.' Seeing the attendant I asked if I could take up the offer. 'Yes, of course,' he replied, 'Where do you want it delivered?' 'Just leave it where it is,' was my reply. It was just what we needed and we festooned it with posters and goods which caught the attention of people on the escalator.

Banners along the stairways and posters at all the entrances of the shopping centre attracted thousands of visitors to the Rich Fool grotto. Send the Light Trust provided us with a large book exhibition; Scripture Gift Mission gave us Scripture portions in many languages and Gospel Recordings did likewise with records. The BCM had its own exhibition promoting the mission. The venture led to many otherwise unreached people hearing the gospel, and was a commercial success. It also put the Birmingham City Mission very much in the public eye. We were becoming an effective force for God in the midst of the city.

Going to the people

Exhibition evangelism is an effective means of reaching people in our modern world. The indoor shopping precincts in many of our new towns lend themselves to this type of work. It is a case of putting the message where the people are in a language they understand. Moreover, it is a one-to-one personal matter. The environment is not churchy or religious but familiar and relaxed. Shoppers are used to browsing, and if the exhibits are brightly lit, colourful and tastefully arranged, people will pause to look and ask questions. It is a method which seems to attract more voluntary helpers. This may be because the shifts are short and easily defined—usually four hours—at times to suit the helper. The wide variety of skills necessary also creates an unusual opportunity for people to use their talents. Of course, standards of presentation, decor, cleanliness, tidiness and the personal appearance of volunteers must be high. Prior training and prayer times are essential, as is an adequate follow-up procedure.

Since the Rich Fool exhibition, the BCM has produced several others. There was 'The World's Greatest Treasure', a kind of Bible exhibition, but presented in such a way that families out shopping queued up to see it. It was accompanied by good sales of Bibles in modern English.

Easter exhibitions have also been held promoting books such as Michael Green's *The Day Death Died*. In recent years continuous video showings of the film *Jesus* have attracted the attention of passers-by. On these occasions the display of an Easter garden has been a central feature.

In March 1985 an excellent exhibition on the theme 'God Cares' was held in the Birmingham Shopping Centre, the place which refused our application in 1977. At this exhibition we were not allowed to sell anything, but as it was in the main thoroughfare leading to the chief railway station it was seen by large numbers of people. A great deal of personal counselling took place, which led to several conversions. All the visuals were made by our own staff. The design, photography and lettering were so good that a passer-by who was a professional exhibitor asked which company had done the work.

As the exhibition area was very large we were able to arrange the displays like the spokes of a wheel. At the hub was the counselling area, with tables and chairs beneath a canopy, and beside it a tower display 'God Cares' poster. Each display section had its own theme, such as, 'God Cares for the Homeless', 'God Cares for the Elderly', and so on through all the facets of the mission's ministry. At the far extremities continuous audio visual presentations attracted passers-by to watch videos and slides on the BCM or Bible themes, or listen to the preaching of Billy Graham.

It was at this time that we developed the use of the outstretched hands as the BCM motif. Originally Richard Grundy, our graphic designer, had thought of this symbol representing the outstretched hands of Jesus. Now we came to see it as God reaching out through us to care for mankind. One hand represents the proclamation of the gospel—teaching, beckoning, warning and pointing the way. The other hand represents the practical aspects of the gospel—lifting, touching, reaching, defending and supporting.

A right balance between practical and spiritual care is the secret of effectiveness for city missions. The world at large judges us by what we do rather than by what we say. Faith without works is dead, but works without faith is equally dead. We act according to what we believe and what we believe depends upon the information we receive. Practising and proclaiming are therefore of equal importance. Exhibition evangelism is a method of reaching out with both hands to a modern world.

11

A Hostel For The Homeless

'HAVE YOU HEARD THE NEWS? There's been a fire at the crypt. The men have been put into the street and they have nowhere to go.' Margaret's face showed deep concern as she spoke. I looked out of the window. Snow lay on the ground on that cold, grey January morning. 'Can we do anything for them?' she continued. After pausing for thought I replied, 'Let's call the staff together for prayer this afternoon and we'll see what we can do.'

As we gathered later in the upper-floor lounge someone produced a newspaper. There was a full report of the fire. St Chad's Roman Catholic Cathedral had for several years provided a refuge for down-and-outs in its crypt. The men slept on mattresses on the floor. Someone had fallen asleep while smoking, and that had led to a fire and the deaths of two of the men. The city's hostels were full. In any case, these men were mainly banned from hostels because of violent and drunken behaviour. No one wanted them. Many of them frequented our soup kitchen, but left early because they were required to be in the crypt by nine-thirty if they wanted a bed.

Having brought the matter to God in prayer we discussed our course of action. We decided that we would be prepared to stay open all night, but first we would put the matter to the test. Nothing was said to the men in the soup kitchen. They had their normal handouts of soup, sandwiches and tea. As usual a film was shown—one about the building of the Forth Bridge, from the Shell Library. At nine o'clock there was a call for quiet, and in the smoky atmosphere of the room the Bible was quietly read and explained; this was followed by a short prayer. The men were attentive and unusually quiet. Following this it was usual for people to leave for the crypt, but no one moved. 'How many of you have nowhere to sleep tonight?' I asked. About thirty men put up their hands. They were a sorry bunch, unshaven, dirty, clad in an assortment of clothing which was either too big or too small. Some grinned with the unreal geniality of the alcoholic still under the influence, but most were pale, silent and morose. As they huddled near the stoves that cold, frosty night it was clear that they were in no hurry to leave.

'If you have no other place to go to you can stay here,' I announced. 'We have no beds but you can sleep in the chairs or on the floor.'

A fresh cup of tea was made for everyone while staff busied themselves in the warehouse above, looking for any suitable clothing to serve as bedding. An assortment of old blankets, overcoats and sweaters was found and handed out. Our first night shelter had begun.

Each night the exercise was repeated. Rotas were formed for the staff, one of whom offered to bed down with the men. A simple breakfast was prepared in the mornings and the place was cleaned up and given an airing. It was hard work and there were casualties. I was one. Having worked throughout the day it had been my turn to be on duty all night, too. I had taken some rest by lying on the floor of my office, but I was cold. When morning came I was glad to go home to catch an hour or two's sleep before returning to work. On rising from bed, however, I was struck with excruciating pain. It was my first experience of sciatica and was to keep me in bed for ten weeks.

In spite of the staff's marvellous work we realised that we could not go on indefinitely providing overnight accommodation at the centre. We had, however, set in motion an activity which was to become an integral part of the mission. It had also brought the mission to the attention of the authorities. One day I had a phone call from a city councillor. She asked if she and a colleague—a magistrate—could visit us to see what we were doing for these homeless men. When they came I confessed that we had no planning permission and that we were probably contravening fire and health regulations, but that it would be better for them to risk dying in the warmth of our mission that to die in the cold outside. After they had inspected our emergency night shelter they expressed admiration. 'While we have been debating the problems for weeks in the council chamber,' they said, 'you have been doing the work. How can we help you?' A few hours later we were receiving stocks of blankets and mattresses, and a small grant to help us with expenses.

As Easter drew near the weather began to improve and we decided that it was time to close the shelter. The staff had worked valiantly but they were exhausted as this work was in addition to their normal routine. We had made many friends and had come to understand the problems of the single homeless in the best way possible—by sharing their suffering and identifying with them. From now on we would endeavour to find a permanent emergency night shelter where we could continue to minister to their bodies and souls.

'Your offer is accepted'

Two young men sat in my office outlining their plans and asking for advice and counsel. They had both been made redundant from their jobs as fund-raisers for Dr Barnardo's Homes and were seeking a new role for themselves in which they could use their gifts. Their idea was to form a consultancy in which they could assist busy Christian workers by helping to raise funds and undertaking the time-consuming business of negotiating with large corporations. Birmingham Christian Projects would be their title. 'I think it's an excellent idea,' I said, 'and I think I have a project here to get you started.'

On my desk was a note from Margaret Anderson, our welfare worker in the soup kitchen. It questioned if I knew that the Church Army Hostel in Granville Street was closing and likely to be sold to Davenports Brewery next door. 'Would you like to check this out and look into the possibilities of the BCM buying it instead?' I asked.

A couple of days later, Peter Combellack returned to tell me that it was indeed true, that he had spoken to an official who was embarrassed by the enquiry. It was to be sold to be turned into a recreation centre for the brewery for a paltry £20,000. Hearing this made me angry. I knew that each night men were sleeping rough and that closure of the hostel would make matters worse. Moreover, I knew that most of the men's problems were caused by alcohol and I was angry to think that the brewing industry would benefit at their expense and pay so little for it into the bargain.

Peter was therefore sent back again to discover if the transaction had been carried out and also convey my feelings about the matter. He returned to say that contracts had not been exchanged and that the Church Army would far rather the mission buy the hostel as a going concern and not sell to the brewers. Knowing the agreed price, but hearing they would prefer the BCM to keep the work going, I offered less—£16,000 to be exact. The offer was accepted!

This was an incredibly low price for a building in the heart of the city. It is within walking distance of Birmingham Town Hall, and large enough to accommodate over eighty men. Cheap as it was, it was dear for us, because we had no money. We were about to witness yet another miracle.

The question of cash

Soon small gifts began to arrive earmarked for the new
hostel. One evening I had to attend a prearranged meeting in
a home. An entry had been made in my diary, but I had no
idea what the meeting was for. When I arrived I discovered it
was a meeting of trustees of a local charity. They said they
had money to disburse, but that it must be given to an
evangelical group engaged in residential care of drug addicts,
alcoholics and the like. When the original appointment was
made we had no such residential work. That evening I was
able to announce that we had agreed to buy the hostel. I left
with a cheque for £3,000.

A stranger called in at our Bromsgrove Street shop asking
for me. He told me that he was a representative of the
landlords who owned the premises in which we stood. A
director of the company had seen a press report of the work
we did there—possibly the emergency night shelter—and
discovering they owned the property the board had decided
to allow us to occupy it rent free for the next few years. At
that time we were paying over £1,000 per annum for 36
Bromsgrove Street. As we had agreed to pay £16,000 for the
Granville Street Hostel, which was on a sixteen-year lease, I
reckoned that the £1,000 a year rent relief was just what we
needed. In practice it had little bearing on the situation other
than to give us much needed encouragement for our faith at
that precise time. We were to pay no more rent after 30
September, the very date the Church Army had asked us to
complete the purchase.

Peter Combellack and I visited the London headquarters
of the Church Army to make final arrangements. We agreed
to pay an extra £2,000 for the furniture, fixtures and fittings.
We needed another £13,000 immediately, and applied for a
mortgage from the city council. After all, we were providing
a service to the community. It would cost the authorities a
great deal of money if the forty residents in the hostel had to
be re-housed by them. Fortunately the mission's charitable

status and integrity had been validated by civil servants when the BCM applied for a mortgage to buy a house for students some months earlier. This loan had taken so long to obtain that the property had been sold to another buyer. So this time we asked our bank manager for a bridging loan. However, he would not provide one unless the Housing Department gave a written assurance that a mortgage would be forthcoming. When I requested this I was merely offered an appointment to discuss the matter two weeks later. Time was pressing. The exchange of contracts was due. I therefore went to Bush House where the department was housed. Obtaining the room and floor number of the official concerned, I pushed past several security men and burst into his office unannounced. I made quite clear the urgency of the business and refused to leave without a letter to the bank. Triumphant, I returned with it in my hand, the bank manager released the money and the hostel was ours.

Finding the money to buy the hostel was one thing, finding the men to run it was another. We advertised and prayed. By the time we actually took over its administration in November 1979 we were still without an experienced manager. When I visited the hostel a few days earlier, however, the Church Army warden told me he was having difficulty with his move to Ireland and asked if he could stay on in his quarters for a few weeks. In exchange, he would continue to run the hostel. God had answered our prayers. By the time he was ready to leave we had employed both a manager and an assistant. Moreover, the delay had allowed us to feel our way in without causing upheaval among the residents.

A place to stay

During the period of negotiation I visited the hostel and met one of the residents, Roland, whom I had known for many years. He was a road sweeper for the council and often worked in the Bull Ring. Dressed in smart blue overalls and his uniform cap he would propel his brightly painted yellow barrow towards our open-air meeting. Then he would stand leaning on his broom, listening to the preacher declaring the Word of God. In personal conversations afterwards he showed a serious interest.

Roland looked very gloomy on that day I saw him in the hostel. 'Mr Orton,' he groaned, 'What are we going to do? They are going to close the hostel and we have nowhere to go.'

I knew he had lived there for many years and that he had no relatives and few friends. 'That is why I am here,' I told him. 'The mission is going to take the hostel over and you will be able to stay.' With tears in his eyes he said, 'That's the best news I've heard for years.'

Roland did stay until a year or so later he developed cancer. He was somewhat fearful of death but I was able to talk to him about the Saviour and the glorious future which awaits those who trust Him. I told him the chorus we used to teach the children, 'Away far beyond Jordan, we'll meet in that land, O won't it be grand! If you get there before I do, look out for me, I'm coming too.'

A few days later he called me to him and said, 'It's all right now, I'll be looking out for you.' Not long afterwards I was called upon to conduct his funeral, which I did with a sense of joy.

Money no object!

A month after we had taken over the running of the hostel I received a phone call in my office. A local architect rang asking if I could call upon him right away as he had some business to attend to which was very important for me. When I arrived, he and his colleagues were poring over building plans in their drawing office.

'These are plans for renovating your hostel in Granville Street,' he started. 'We want your permission to go ahead.'

'Wherever would the money come from?' I queried as I viewed the extent of the work proposed.

'Money is no object!' he went on. 'That is not your concern.'

'Then I give you my permission,' was my immediate response.

We talked for a while about light wells, bathrooms, a new roof, central heating and a thousand and one other ideas for refurbishment. Soon more fundamental ideas emerged.

'Can I have a night shelter for women?' was one of my questions. Some months earlier, I recollected, a young woman had come hungry to our soup kitchen. She was obviously in distress and had nowhere to go. We learned that she had fled from home some months earlier and had gone to live in London. There she had been involved with the seamy side of life, including some drug addiction. Seeing a friend dying of heroin poisoning she had become very frightened and run back to her home city. But where could she turn? She had no money and nowhere to stay. I did my best to help, offering to contact her parents to try to persuade them to take her back. Because she had left her belongings at a very dingy down-town pub she needed to collect them.

Jean Robb, my secretary, accompanied her as far as the door of the pub and waited, but she did not return. Jean came back to fetch me so we could see if we could find the missing girl. As we peered around that smoke-filled, evil-smelling place, full of pimps, pushers, prostitutes and the like, I felt so sad that we had no refuge to which the girl could have been taken immediately.

Other women and girls had been brought to us also. Two fifteen-year-olds had been found sleeping in public toilets. Fortunately we were able to reunite them with their families. Several times our workers had put up camp beds in their own homes for such people. 'Yes,' I thought, 'We must have a night shelter for women.'

'Could we have a medical wing?' was another of my

requests. The case of Jimmy, the Irish tinker, came to mind. There must be many others like him who, when discharged from hospital, have nowhere to go. Jimmy had been coming to our mission for years. He possessed a set of drain rods and would go around asking people if he could clean their drains. He didn't draw social security, but would live on his wits. However, he was an alcoholic. One day while in a drunken stupor he had fallen and broken his thigh. In due course he was discharged from hospital with his leg in plaster up to his waist, walking on crutches. His only home was a derelict house, which was his 'skipper'. There he existed, with news-papers and bits of carpet to keep him warm as he slept on a solid bit of floor, amidst the broken floorboards.

One day Jimmy had been drinking again and had fallen outside the Ice Rink near our mission. A police patrol had stopped, and receiving the customary drunken abuse from the Irishman, had decided to arrest him. Two policemen were trying to put him, complete with leg plaster and crutches, into their panda car. I crossed the road to offer assistance.

'What's he done and where are you taking him?' I asked.

'He's drunk and disorderly and we're taking him to Dig-beth Police Station,' stated the constable.

'What will happen there?'

'He'll be charged and put in a cell until morning.'

'Will there be a bed there?'

'Yes, of course.'

'Good, he hasn't got a bed, and with a leg like that he ought to have one. Will you give him any food?'

'Yes, of course.'

'Good, he hasn't had a good meal since he left hospital. What will happen tomorrow?'

'He'll be taken to court to appear before the magistrate and fined.'

'He's got no money, so what will happen then?'

'He'll be given seven days in Winson Green prison.'

'Have they got beds there?'

'Yes, of course.'

'Good, with that leg he ought to rest up a bit. Will they give him any food?'

By this time the policeman's face was becoming purple. 'Who are you anyway?' he demanded.

'I am the city missionary from across the road. I know this man well, he was on his way to our soup kitchen,' I answered.

'Look here,' he said, addressing Jimmy, 'Do you want to come with us or go with him?'

Jimmy elected to come with me, and somehow I half carried him to the mission and down the alley-way to his familiar seat in the soup kitchen.

There was a sequel to this incident. Some months later we were holding an open-air meeting in the Bull Ring and I was preaching from the rostrum. Two drunks were attacking me, trying to punch me and knock me off the platform. Suddenly Jimmy appeared, no longer needing plaster or crutches. With fists flying he laid into the drunks, then taking hold of the rostrum with one hand he stood with the other fist clenched, and said to me, 'You go on preaching and I'll fight them off!'

Thinking about Jimmy and many others like him, who needed a bed when they were sick and homeless, I repeated my request, 'Could we have a medical wing?'

Now where was all this money which would be needed to renovate the hostel building coming from? It was some time before I found the answer to that question. You will remember that we had applied to the council for a mortgage and that in the meantime we obtained a loan from the bank. It appears that Birmingham City Council had at that time underspent its budget based on the grants which central government paid out for the benefit of the inner city. If the money was not used in the financial year ending in March it would be lost and the following year's budget would also be reduced. Instructions were therefore given that some appropriate use for the money must be found immediately. When officials of the Housing Department looked in their files, there on the top was Birmingham City Mission's application for a mortgage for its hostel. Since the mission hostel was so close to Bush House, home of the department, someone was sent round straight away to look at it. At first they said that the place was only fit for demolition, but when the architect saw it he realised its potential and drew up the plans which he showed me. The authorities were prepared to pay for all the work, including complete renewal of furniture, bedding, office equipment, right down to crockery and cutlery.

The final bill amounted to £300,000. When I heard about it I asked what would become of my request for a mortgage on the money we owed the bank. We were simply sent a cheque to repay the bank loan! All this happened without our asking. With God all things are possible.

Making old men new

Our interest in obtaining a hostel was more than simply to help the single homeless whom we knew to be in need. We wanted it to be more than a roof over their heads, because we knew that there were deeper needs than purely the physical. In providing clothing we always felt it was more important to put a new man in old clothing rather than an old man in new clothing. The man is more important than the things which he possesses. So in providing a hostel we were thinking too of the spiritual dimension which could lead to conversion. An encounter with Jesus would therefore be necessary, so Christian staff, prayer, Bible reading and loving care would be essential.

A year of renovation

We did not realise what other things we were taking on, however. In order to finance the daily running of the hostel we had to operate efficient financial practices. Charges were made to residents, which were passed on to the Department of Health and Social Security (DHSS). Budgets had to be worked out for food, laundry, heat and light, cleaning materials, staff wages and so on. Suddenly we realised that it was like running a hotel and that we needed to register for Value Added Tax (VAT). At first we tried to keep this to the hostel alone, but government officials insisted that the whole of the BCM be registered. Later that worked to our advantage, for the amount of VAT we recovered on the rebuilding project was sufficient to buy the mission a much needed vehicle, a large parcel van.

When we were to receive funding for the renovations it was necessary to draw up a contract with the city council. As we were a registered charity we first had to get permission from the Charity Commissioners. This process usually takes many months, but we were short of time. Our solicitor worked very hard on our behalf and the mission staff prayed much about it. We were on retreat at Felixstowe when the solicitor rang to say we could go ahead, but he needed my signature. He suggested we meet half-way, so I drove to Newport Pagnell motorway service station and he joined me from Birmingham. In the back of his car I signed the agreement which released the money and allowed the renovation work to proceed.

The actual building work could not be completed in less than a year, but the final plans were finished and contracts signed immediately. Furniture and equipment were purchased and put into storage. This included hundreds of blankets, sheets, pillowcases, mattresses, kitchen utensils, crockery and cutlery. The builders arrived. Throughout the whole operation we did not have less than thirty residents who needed to be fed and bedded. It was necessary, therefore, to work on one section at a time, and when one was completed move the men into that. When the kitchen was being rebuilt we constructed a temporary one and cooking continued.

Each week a progress meeting was held in the clerk of works' hut on the site. Besides him, architects, contractors, foremen, various experts and myself were involved. At every stage we were consulted about the men's welfare, with special regard to their needs. Even there opportunities occurred for Christian witness. We sensed the presence of God, whose guiding hand was so evident.

Scaffolding poles appeared everywhere. On one occasion we were very glad of them.

The low wing had once been a bakery. It had been converted into a single-storey hostel made up of small cubicles separated by partitions and doors, such as one might find at a public swimming bath, easy to climb over or crawl under. The only heating consisted of a hot-water pipe high in the roof. This unit was turned into a two-storey night shelter, with room for sixteen beds on the first floor and sixteen on the ground floor, eight for men and eight for women, in a self-contained private section. The extra floor and the new roof, central heating and bathrooms proved to be too heavy for the old walls. They began to bulge and soon it was noticed that the scaffolding was actually propping them up. A steel cage was devised to give support from within, resulting in a considerable difference between the dimensions of the outer walls and inner living space.

Building work always creates dust, noise and confusion. Having a large reconstruction project taking place around them was very trying to our residents, but it was better than being out on the streets, and many had experienced that. They appreciated that the work was for their benefit and that we could have closed, but preferred to provide them with shelter.

One morning a man was reported missing. He had not been in bed, which was unusual for him. For some it was a common occurrence, either because of heavy drinking or because they had found somewhere else to stay. This man had lived in the hostel for a long time, kept himself to himself and never caused any trouble, was upright and clean, but silent and alone. We were concerned about this sixty-year-old Scot so we checked around the hospitals and finally reported his absence to the police. There was no sign of him and his belongings were still beside the bed.

Two days later the construction work was in full swing. Amidst the noise of trucks and cement mixers, nailing and hammering, I met the foreman and reported to him a complaint from our men. They had been transferred to the new night shelter, but could not gain access to the toilets in the new block. I asked when they would be ready for use. He assured me they were already available and to confirm it he led me to them. They appeared to be locked, so he produced a screwdriver and showed me that the locks could easily be released from the outside in case anyone locked himself in. He opened the door and to our shock and horror the body of the man we had lost fell out at our feet.

The foreman's face turned so ashen white I thought he would faint, so I sent him hurrying to find the hostel manager while I stood guard over the body, calling to the men upstairs to remain in their room for a while. Soon we had a doctor and the police with us and matters were taken out of our hands. The man had died of natural causes and we could not have helped him at the time of his seizure. Once again we were aware of the importance of our work in seeking the least, the last and the lost. Eventually we discovered that the Scot had one next of kin, an elderly sister too frail to travel, who lived alone in Edinburgh. From her we learned that her brother had served as a soldier in Burma in World War II, and that he had won medals for his bravery. As I conducted his funeral, attended by our staff and a few of our residents, I praised God that we had been able to care for him and show by deeds and words that God loved him.

Major alterations took place in the hostel's high wing. On

the ground floor had been situated the only baths and toilets in the building. They were very primitive, rather like those of an old Victorian railway station. These were demolished to make way for the medical unit, while modern bathrooms and toilets were constructed at convenient places around the hostel.

The rather draughty lounge, with its high ceiling, bare walls, antiquated lighting and broken furniture, gave way to a modern, warm, well-lit, carpeted room with modern chairs. There had been a small chapel next to the lounge. Some men complained that we committed sacrilege when this was demolished to make room for staff offices—not that they had attended services, but it had been used by the old stagers as a quiet smoking room. Our motive for making this change was to ensure that all the men attended services by holding them occasionally in the main lounge. This has worked in practice as most people's dislike for religion is due to prejudice rather than experience.

Additional comforts for the residents were provided in the form of snooker and pool tables, darts, colour television and hot drinks machines. The basement, which had been just a store for rubbish, was turned into workshops for those interested in using their time to practical advantage. It was fitted out with work benches, cutting and drilling machines, and a variety of hand tools for wood or metal work.

The first floor of the high wing had been one huge, draughty, open dormitory, with the customary high ceiling and one-pipe heating system. The second floor contained tiny cubicles similar to those in the low wing. No ceiling existed; one could see right up into the gabled roof. As the whole building backed on to a factory wall, daylight entered from one side only, which would limit any newly constructed room to permanent artificial lighting. The architect had foreseen this and therefore removed part of the roof in two areas to make light wells around which comfortable bedrooms were built. The wells were tastefully clad with timber, giving a kind of Swiss chalet atmosphere to rooms far from the outer walls of the building. The two floors contained sixteen rooms each, plus modern bathrooms and toilets. Ceilings were lowered, and contemporary lighting installed.

Each room now had its own unbreakable wash basin, with hot and cold water, wooden bed with interior-sprung mattress, wardrobe and locker. Hot-water radiators and carpeted floors made them warm. Small-pane metal windows gave place to large, airy wooden ones with brightly patterned curtains. Colour schemes differ from room to room to minimise the sense of institutionalism. Finally, each bed was covered with a hand-knitted bedspread made by the loving hands of local Christians.

By the spring of 1981 the work was completed, and a service of dedication of the newly renovated hostel was held. Mrs Jill Knight, the local MP, Mrs Edwina Currie, who was then a prominent city councillor, and a number of other local dignitaries attended. Architects, builders, police officers, probation officers, social workers and many others were there, including the officials from the Housing Department, who had thought the building was only worth demolishing, and the bank manager who had hesitated to loan us a few thousand pounds. BCM trustees, committee members and staff were present, as were a number of our residents. The Revd David MacInnes, from the Cathedral, took this opportunity to deliver an excellent gospel message to the whole assembly. The entire building was open for inspection and refreshment provided. There was a tremendous sense of the presence of God as we sang His praise for the glorious miracles which we had witnessed in the purchase and renovation of the hostel and in the lives of those who had come to work and live there.

12

BCM Charity Shops

'OYEZ! OYEZ! Hear ye, hear ye!' boomed the loud voice of the big-framed, large-booted town crier, dressed in scarlet cape and three-cornered hat. Standing on the blue-brick platform, holding a large bell, he cried out again, 'Com visit the new shoppe in Bell Court this very day.' Shakespeare's town resounded again, but not to *Hamlet* or *Macbeth*, nor was it *Much Ado About Nothing*. The town crier was none other than Mark Lacey, the new extension secretary of the BCM. But why was he so far from Birmingham? Was this some midsummer night's dream or a winter's tale? No, he really was in Stratford-upon-Avon, but as the result of a mistake.

Mark had joined us earlier in the year (1981). Not that he had planned to do so, in fact even that was a kind of accident. His business in the jewellery trade was a far cry from city mission work, but for some time he had been restless, not quite sure why, but sensing it was time to change. One morning a client cancelled an appointment and Mark sat at home undecided what to do next. Beside him he noticed a magazine passed to him recently but still unread. Gradually, as he perused its pages, he realised that he was at a turning point in his life. This BCM outreach magazine challenged and inspired him. As soon as his wife returned home he took her by the hand, led her to the car and drove to Bromsgrove Street. That was the beginning of the process which led to him becoming our extension secretary.

This is how Mark told his own story in a later edition of the BCM magazine:

Was it by advertising? NO. Was it by asking round the churches? NO. Was it by recommendation? NO. Then how? By prayer. Not the prayers of one person, but by the BCM and their prayer partners as a whole. My coming to the mission was not only a triumph in answered prayer by BCM prayer partners, but also an answer to the prayers of my wife and me. The BCM had been praying for over twelve months for this rare and nearly extinct creature to turn up. We ourselves had had godly desires to serve Christ full time for over twelve months. During this period we had many experiences of God dealing with us. In family business and spiritual life the Lord had led us through paths which were not of our choosing, yet which gave us important lessons for the future. We now know that God was training us for His service.

In the first week of October 1980 in a hotel bedroom in Hull I again asked God if He would release me for His service. He gave the answer and a promise in Jeremiah 52 vv.31–34: 'in the twelfth month on the twenty-fifth day...the King of Babylon lifted up the head of Jehoiachin King Judah and brought him out of prison.'

So with a date and a promise that He would provide all, I asked Him to guide me.

A dear Christian sister from my church called at my house soon after with the BCM magazine for my wife and me, as she put it, 'to read and pray about'. We did and God spoke again. 'This is the way, walk ye in it.' After much prayer and asking God to open up the way we visited the BCM head-quarters. We had made no appointment and did not know of the vacancy for extension secretary, but asked God for two things. First, that Mr Orton would be there and able to see us and, second, that he would say something that would speak loudly to us.

God answered our request and also revealed the actual nature of our service.

The job description Mr Orton showed me put together so wonderfully all my spiritual desires and abilities. My business experience would be a great help and my hobbies an asset. What could I do other than bow to the Lord's will and answer His call to work in the BCM immediately after Christmas. Thus the text given in Hull that night was fulfilled. Since our coming we have also seen the fulfilment of the last two verses in the passage, food and clothing being supplied through the gifts of God's children.

Now Mark had been given his first assignment—to find a vacant shop which could be used as a short-term charity shop. He went about it in his usual cheerful, enthusiastic manner. Armed with the request that we find a shop on the Stratford Road, a main road leading out from the centre of Birmingham, he pestered a number of estate agents. In response we received the address of No. 9 Bell Court. Immediately we went in search of this place but couldn't find it; it was not even on our maps. Back to the agents we went, only to be told that Bell Court was in Stratford-upon-Avon, twenty miles south of Birmingham. No wonder we couldn't find it! We did go to see the shop, however, and it was in such a good situation and in such fine condition that we took the letting for three months.

Sortie into Shakespeare country

BCM workers had visited Stratford-upon-Avon on a couple of occasions before. They had been based at the West Street Mission Hall, a small centre led by a retired railwayman. This man used to pass Bromsgrove Street and became a prayer partner of the BCM. Eventually he invited us to his town, for which he had a great burden. One Saturday a team arrived on the very day a new traffic experiment was launched, in which vehicles were excluded from the shopping precinct. It was ideal for our purpose, and as workers began distributing Christian tracts others put up a small book table. As I fixed some gospel posters to the table I remarked that it would not be long before someone asked if we had permission to do this. Before I could straighten up a voice behind me said, 'Have you got permission to do this?'

'Why, do I need permission?' I asked innocently. 'And who are you?'

The man dressed in a smart suit towered above me. 'I am the Chief Constable,' he said stiffly, 'and as this is the first day of our new traffic arrangements I am here to make sure all is well. Now suppose an ambulance or fire engine wants to come through here, you will be causing an obstruction.'

Past experience had taught me to make sure that we didn't cause an obstruction or create a nuisance. I pointed out to the officer that the table had been placed beside a wooden bench and stone flower pot put in position by council workers and that in no way could we be causing an obstruction. Also, I asked him if Christian workers were more of a problem than the vandals and petty criminals in the town. Muttering something about getting permission on another occasion he quietly walked away, leaving us to get on with evangelising.

At lunch time I asked the railwayman if open-air preaching was done in the town. He replied that it was not because when they had asked permission it had been refused. But that was seventeen years before! That afternoon we began to preach and soon a very large crowd gathered.

Inevitably, a policeman arrived with his walkie-talkie. As I was in charge he was propelled towards me. Fearing that this time we were about to be moved on I asked, 'Do you want to speak to me constable?' 'Yes,' he replied, 'We had a report that your meeting was being disturbed by some drunks. However, I can't see any, so carry on, I'll stay around in case of any trouble.' Once again, God was with us.

Open for business

Now that we had obtained the charity shop we decided to launch it in style. Mark was asked to go to the theatre hire shop for the town crier's outfit. So, here he was announcing, 'Oyez, Oyez, hear ye, hear ye!'

During our three months of residence in Stratford-upon-Avon we took the opportunity to do door-to-door evangelism, and visited every home in the town. Furthermore, a large quantity of Christian books was sold in the shop, which was well set out with Tearcraft goods and nearly new clothing. Although we didn't make much profit, the venture paid for itself and was wholly successful. Finally, we hired the beautiful Town Hall, with its lovely chandeliers and oil paintings, and there in the dance hall showed Billy Graham films to a good audience of local people.

Choosing the right time to close a work is just as important as opening one. Running a shop in Stratford-upon-Avon, when our offices were in the centre of Birmingham, created a number of difficulties, and our staff had been overstretched. We made it a matter of prayer and finally agreed the time had come to close the Stratford charity shop. It had been very worthwhile—many had been reached with the gospel, local Christians had been encouraged and much useful experience had been gained. A letter was sent to the agents giving 23 May as the closing date. The very next day we received a letter from the agents, which had crossed with ours, saying that they were sorry but the temporary lease would have to cease on 23 May!

Hidden profit

Having had a taste of success in charity shop work we looked for another opportunity. The primary reason for doing so was not to raise funds, as is the case with shops run by Oxfam or Dr Barnardo's. Although we welcomed the chance to turn goods given to us into cash for use in evangelism, we had discovered that here was a means of reaching people with the good news and also of building up a relationship with them which could lead to an ongoing counselling and caring situation. Most churches are closed most of the time; they are open for a few hours on Sundays and a little in the week. Church buildings also tend to be rather forbidding to non-churchgoers, because of ornate architecture and unattractive furniture. Often they are built in obscure places or are not easily accessible. Who wants to walk through a graveyard to obtain help in distress? A shop, on the other hand, is open during shop hours on six days a week. It is easily accessible in a parade of retail units selling a variety of goods which attract the customer to the area, and it is natural and unembarrassing for them to pop into the mission shop. There is also an attractiveness about the display and a familiarity which makes them feel at ease. The opportunity therefore exists for conversations which can easily be turned to spiritual account. Once they are interested, enquirers feel free to return again and again for more help, which can be backed up with literature. The charity shop can be a mission hall on the High Street.

With this in mind, we were pleased to receive a request for help from someone who needed to dispose of a shop lease. He was a Christian man who had run a chemist's shop for some years, but through ill health and declining business wished to retire. The premises were situated in a parade on a busy bus route in Ward End, on the east side of the city. A few hundred yards away we had acquired a house in which we accommodated some of our students. Their leader, Barry Robinson, was married at about this time. He lived in the house and became the district missionary for Ward End, but used the shop as his base, an arrangement which worked well in every way and led to a number of local people coming to faith in Christ.

Another charity shop was opened in 1982 in Bearwood, on the west side of the city. The shop was for sale, but as it was vacant we applied to use it temporarily until a buyer was found. This arrangement lasted for five months and was an effective witness in a busy shopping area, and also an encouragement and a means of service for many local believers.

One unexpected bonus of opening the Bearwood shop was that we were supplied with almost all the office furniture we needed for the new headquarters at Arden Road. Having obtained permission to use the shop, but not yet moved in, we put a poster in the window announcing its opening. Mark had the keys to the building and needed to go there one day to admit the electrician. The poster had already done its work for on the doorstep Mark found sacks of donated clothing. One of these contained ladies' underwear.

Later in the day a very large woman came in to look around and asked if we had any 'foundation bits'! Remembering the appropriate sack Mark searched and found an extra large bra which in spite of embarrassment proved to be just what was required. Next the matter of price was discussed.

'Can't afford it, love,' she said sadly, and clearly she couldn't.

'You're like me,' said Mark, 'I can't afford robes of righteousness to enter heaven, but the Lord gives them free.'

'Oh, I don't need them,' she chuckled, 'I ain't going there!'

After further spiritual conversation Mark not only gave her the garment she wanted but the rest of the outsize clothing in the sack as well, plus a pile of handbills about the charity shop. At this she offered to kiss him and said she would give the leaflets to the members of her club.

A few days later the woman was in the shop again and was persuaded to buy a small cheap Bible.

A week later she returned again with the Bible in her hand. Mark feared that she had a complaint but was overjoyed to hear her ask if she could have thirty such Bibles. It transpired that the lady's club had been started in a small lounge, but numbers had grown and it had become necessary to build an extension. A little dedication meeting for this was to be held and they wanted to give Bibles to the ladies who would be there.

Mark obtained the Bibles and was present at the meeting to 'cut the tape' for the new extension. He also took the opportunity to pass on a clear gospel message.

This contact led to him being invited to other meetings, including a gentlemen's supper club. Here he was requested to speak about the work of the mission and answer questions. Afterwards a gentleman approached him and asked if the mission could do with any office furniture. His company was closing down a factory and offices and would be willing to donate any of the contents we required.

We had just bought the Arden Road centre but the offices were bare. When our truck returned from the Redditch factory we had all the furniture we needed.

And it all started with a large lady asking for 'foundation bits'!

13

Literature Distribution

I OWE MY CONVERSION to Christ largely to a book which I read in the spring of 1945, *The Triumph of John and Betty Stam*, which was written by Mrs Howard Taylor and published by the China Inland Mission. Not only did it lead to my conversion, but it has influenced me all these years in matters of prayer, faith and world evangelisation. It has also convinced me of the power and importance of the written word.

Literature evangelism is a must for city mission work. The Birmingham Town Mission published in its reports for 1865 that their Bible women had sold:

Numbers of Books Sold
- Bibles 168
- Gospels 19
- Testaments 285
- Prayer Books 98
- Psalms 71
- Hymn Books 8
- Miscellaneous Publications 271

Two of the Bible Women, accompanied by a Missionary

who has occupied part of his time in open-air addresses, have sold at a stall during the fair week 921 Bibles and Testaments, 273 Prayer Books, and 227 miscellaneous publications.

The above added to the sales of the four previous years gives a total of:

> Copies of the Scripture 4772
> Prayer Books 1146
> Hymn Books 221
> Miscellaneous publications 1317
> *Grand total of all kinds in four years: 7456*

Part of my conversion story is that I was helped by reading a gospel tract which I found on a table in my home. It may have been given to my father or an older brother in a pub and put out on the table as a pocket-emptying exercise. 'Seek first the kingdom of God and His righteousness, and all these things shall be yours' (Mt 6:33) is a text which is burned for ever into my mind because these words on the tract caused me to begin reading the Bible.

Books and tracts have therefore had a high priority with BCM from its beginning. Eric Williams, secretary of the Evangelical Tract Society, joined the mission's advisory council and supplied large quantities of literature, looking to God to supply the funds to pay for them. He was a man of prayer and faith who could relate countless stories of people converted through his tracts. Birmingham was the birthplace of the Scripture Gift Mission, which supplied us with not only literature in many languages but also a display unit to be exhibited in an illuminated showcase in a city subway. The Pocket Testament League also started in Birmingham, founded by Helen Cadbury, later Mrs Alexander Dixon, when she was seventeen. To mark her ninetieth birthday she launched a distribution of gospels throughout the city at a public meeting at which she spoke eloquently. Many thousands of these gospels were given out by the BCM.

For several years the mission used a car trailer, supplied by the Good News Trailer Mission, as a mobile bookstall.

This became a focal point for 'Gospel Raids', when voluntary workers would sell books, give out tracts, preach in the street and engage in door-to-door personal evangelism in a spiritually deprived area.

Birmingham's rag market is famous for the variety of cheap goods available. In recent years it has become more like an Indian bazaar, and in an attempt to reach the Asian community Alan Fleming and Harvey Challoner were asked to obtain a stall. Getting a regular pitch is an elaborate procedure. On each visit one has first to register with the market superintendent and then wait till all the usual stall holders have occupied their places. Then the superintendent walks round the market noting vacant plots. He decides who should occupy them, giving priority to those whose names have appeared most frequently on his register; the rest are turned away. It took about two years for us to be allocated a regular stall of our own, and this has been used each Tuesday for twenty years. The venture is not a paying proposition, but has been an outlet for Christian literature and a point for personal contact in the market place for thousands of needy people of many languages, races, religions and cultural backgrounds.

Earnest enquirers

A seventeen-year-old Asian boy paused at the stall noticing some literature in the Urdu language. He was a strong Muslim, but seriously wanting to know more of the Christian faith. We talked for a while about Jesus and his curiosity was aroused.

'Could you come to speak to us in our Islamic class?' was his amazing request.

'I would love to. Where is it held?' was my reply.

'On Sunday afternoons in a school in Sparkbrook. If you will come I can meet you at the corner of Farm Road and Stratford Road at three o'clock.'

It was a long shot, and my experience told me that an

arrangement made like this after a short conversation with a stranger in the market place on Tuesday was hardly likely to succeed. Nevertheless, I travelled several miles from home and prayed that the boy would turn up. To my relief and joy he was waiting for me.

First we went into a schoolroom, where about twenty young men were playing table tennis. After we had watched for a while we were called upstairs to a room where a carpet was placed for prayer. Following the custom I removed my shoes, but sat on a chair while the others went through the Muslims' prayer ritual. When this was finished I was introduced to the president, who invited me to speak about my faith to the group. I simply told them about myself—how I had been a typical English person who had had little knowledge of God and lived for material things. Then I told them of my discovery of Christ and how He had changed my life and given me peace and joy. Anything controversial I avoided; I just gave them the facts of my experience.

The president then invited questions and the young men were full of them, They treated me with respect and were eager to know more about Christ and the Christian faith. This questioning went on for some time until I thought it wise to bring it to an end, suggesting to the president that they might wish to get on with their normal programme. The Mullah then took over, getting the men to recite the text from the Koran in Arabic, which they did without enthusiasm. Again the president invited questions, but instead of addressing the Mullah, they turned again to me, giving me a wonderful opportunity to share my faith more fully.

Once again I felt it was time to close so I asked the president if I could pass on some gifts. I had with me Bible calendars in Urdu and copies of the *Soon* broadsheet, which contains testimonies of conversion to Christ by Asian people. This was also in Urdu, and I passed the papers first to the president for inspection. He was delighted with them, took them from me and handed them out personally to each person in the room. The rag market was proving its worth.

Sowing the seed

The Bromsgrove Street shop presented us with another outlet for Christian literature. A few books were bought from a local supplier and placed on a table near the door. As these were sold we bought more, claiming a discount and ploughing any profits back into increasing the stock. With small gifts of money and books we continued for two or three years, until in 1973 we opened a literature account with a stock of books worth about £300. Since then we have sold many thousands of pounds' worth of Christian literature, especially Bibles.

At Christmas time, when BCM teams used carol singing in their open-air meetings, we took a small table with books and Bibles for sale. They sold very well and it was gratifying to see members of the public who would never enter a Christian bookshop buying good literature to be used as Christmas gifts. The chosen venue was the High Street, opposite large department stores. Sometimes the police would complain that we were creating an obstruction, though we were at pains not to, and move us on. Once I was threatened with arrest. Then a new by-law was passed allowing us to function if we obtained a permit. This we did and suddenly we were no longer causing an obstruction! These permits have been granted over many years and thousands of books have been sold in these situations.

The value of reading Christian literature cannot be measured but it is of great worth. It is truly a sowing of the seed, one sowing, another reaping, but there are countless examples of a harvest.

For many years, the BCM has used a monthly tabloid Christian newspaper, the *Messenger*, in its regular visitation programme. The paper is also used by other city missions, who find it a valuable tool for evangelism. People look forward to the monthly visit and are glad of the reminder and information which the *Messenger* provides. Some keep the papers in a file, others pass them on to friends, and even send them abroad. At the time of writing about 50,000 copies are distributed by our missionaries each year.

14

Arden Road Centre

'WOULD YOU LIKE TO BUY a church at Acocks Green?' asked Bert Aizlewood, our bookkeeper. 'Now why would I want to buy a church?' was my disinterested reply. Bert had heard that we were looking for premises in which we could house students on our Inservice Training Course. At the time they were in lodgings scattered around the city. That created problems because of our inability to provide transport or adequate supervision. But we didn't need a church and I didn't bother to view it. We had been to see a small nursing home which seemed suitable to us, but someone else bought it first. Some days later Bert said again, 'That church in Acocks Green is still up for sale, would you like to buy it?' 'No, we are looking for a large house to accommodate our students.' 'There's a large empty house opposite the church,' he declared. 'All right, I'll go and see it,' I said without enthusiasm.

The church stood on a quiet corner in an old suburb. Its address—Arden Road—indicated that it had once been in the forest of Arden, which covered most of Warwickshire in the Middle Ages. An old oak still stands in the centre of the road, which also contains Tudor cottages and an ancient water pump. Built in 1908, the church building was originally St Mary's parish church hall, used for recreation and Sunday schools. Later it served as a Pentecostal church, but the congregation had dwindled and the building was now up for sale.

Flint Green House, opposite the church, was vacant and in the care of Birmingham Social Services. It was a large rambling house standing in extensive grounds. On enquiry we discovered that it was no longer for sale. However, the official responsible told us that they had another house which was available. As soon as we saw that, we knew it was just what we were looking for. Although it had not been advertised we found out the asking price, put in a bid and it was accepted. But the house alone was not adequate for our needs so we turned our attention to the church.

The estate agent dealing with the Arden Road church was a Christian man who was eager to show me around. The building was constructed at a time when bricklayers were highly skilled and took pride in their work, and it showed. At the front was a well kept garden full of flowers. Inside were seats for about 200 people and all the necessary furniture, including a beautiful carpet down the centre and in the rear schoolrooms. As the sunshine flooded into that rear room I remembered the office in which Jean, Pat, David and Bert worked. It was small and had no windows. Surely they deserved this lovely, sunny, carpeted room.

Finally we came to discuss the price. I had been inwardly praying about it, thinking about the real value, the possible asking price, and the extent to which my faith would go. We had no money at that time, yet we were negotiating for a mortgage on a house in Flint Green Road which was to cost £30,000.

'I must tell you', said the agent, 'that others are interested in this building and we have to take the highest bid.' I thought for a moment and lifted my heart to God. Though

the premises were obviously worth a great deal more, I felt
my faith at that time would not stretch to more than £40,000.
If someone had bid more we could not take it. 'I suppose you
are not allowed to tell me how much your other clients have
offered?' I ventured. 'Not really,' he answered slowly, 'but it
was £25,000.' Hardly believing my ears I said, 'Well, we can
give you £28,000.' He chuckled and said, 'No, just give us
£26,000.'

We were excited at the prospect of moving our offices
from our poor quarters in the city centre to the pleasant,
tree-lined Arden Road in the suburbs. But what were we to
do with the main church hall? There was the temptation to
restart regular church services, but that was not our policy.
The city mission should not set up churches of its own. Its
business is to reach people not usually in touch with the
church and where possible pass them on to existing local
fellowships. If the mission runs churches its workers are not
free to do the task to which they have been called. Funds
given for that work are likely to be directed into church
property rather than evangelism and social care. Besides, if
the mission runs churches, how can it expect other churches
to give their support? Some can hardly afford to support a
pastor of their own so why should they support a pastor in
another church? No, we could not use the building in Arden
Road for church services.

The Voluntary Projects programme

About this time, the spring of 1983, a Christian businessman
began calling at our centre in Bromsgrove Street. He told me
of his concern for unemployed people, and that he was
aware of the vast numbers currently jobless in Birmingham.
Suddenly I realised that here was a use to which we could put
the church hall. The man got me an appointment with the
Manpower Services Commission in Erdington and soon we
were informed of a scheme for voluntary organisations called
the Voluntary Projects Programme (VPP). Supplied with a

handbook of the aims and principles of the scheme, together with application forms, I returned home to pray over the possibilities.

Under VPP rules funding up to £75,000 could be provided for salaries, equipment and running costs for a suitable project. We proposed to employ a staff of seven to recruit up to a hundred unemployed volunteers who would receive training and work in the community doing practical jobs for the elderly and disabled and others in special need. After a great deal of prayer, negotiation and form-filling our proposal was accepted.

The church hall was divided by partitions into four lecture rooms off a central corridor and a larger area in front of the stage for a dining and meeting room. The kitchen was renovated and equipped so that a catering department could be created and cheap meals provided for the volunteers. Other departments were for commercial studies, typing and office procedures, property repairs—especially carpentry, painting and decorating, and gardening.

Staffing was the most difficult task because the MSC required that all staff engaged should come from the unemployment register. It was interesting to discover that the proportion of Christians who were unemployed was very low compared with non-Christians. However, God was good to us and an able team was found. In order to recruit volunteers a contact worker was engaged. Soon he was able to erect an exhibition in the local public library, which was frequented not only by unemployed people but also elderly folk who needed jobs done for them. Practical social work of this kind caused people to be well disposed towards the BCM and provided many opportunities for spiritual conversations which would not otherwise have occurred. Armed with leaflets about the Community Training Project, missionaries and our student team began systematically to visit the Acocks Green district, and discovered that this scheme was an excellent means of overcoming prejudice and giving access for the gospel.

A young artist, a university graduate, applied for a staff appointment. He qualified in that he was unemployed, and he showed us fine examples of his work besides giving a clear Christian testimony. 'If you are willing to do some painting and decorating,' he was told, 'the job is yours.' He learned fast and led the work of decorating kitchens, bedrooms and lounges which were in advanced stages of .dilapidation. Moveover, he turned his lecture room into an art room, and volunteers into art students. Their work was of such a fine order that the local public library was proud to allow an exhibition of paintings and drawings to emblazon its foyer.

Such activity for the long-term unemployed was extremely therapeutic. Redundancy can have a devastating effect upon a person who has worked in a trade for many years. He not only loses his job, he loses his comrades, his routine, sense of purpose and sense of security. The experience can be depressing in the extreme, and though it is not his fault he many feel ashamed and unwilling to meet people.

The Community Training Project gave such people an opportunity to meet others in the same predicament, thereby rescuing them from isolation. New routines were established with regular working hours, and new skills were acquired. Marked changes were noted in the behaviour of our clients. The depressed and sullen became cheerful and alert. Some openly declared that after months of insomnia they were able to sleep at night.

Soon a new problem presented itself to us. Those who had given up looking for work were now finding jobs! We needed to fill the vacancies in our scheme with more long-term unemployed, and the initial recruiting was always the hardest part. Several hundred people passed through the scheme in this way, and it was lovely to see them not only find work but here and there to find Christ too. In the midst of their untiring efforts, staff were sharing their faith on a personal basis.

The sense of achievement and general well-being was further heightened by the response of the elderly and needy in the community who had jobs done for them. They could not have afforded the work, which was often long overdue. There were some amazing stories and sometimes photographs of 'before and after' incidents. Letters of thanks poured in, besides many small gifts in appreciation. These were from people who were mainly shut in, often very lonely and isolated. Because we were doing practical jobs we were being welcomed into their homes. There were accounts of elderly people using delaying tactics in order to keep our workers a little longer because they had been so delighted with their company. Soon we realised we were opening up an entirely new field of service which must be entered.

The Visiting Service for the Elderly

Our first step was taken at Christmas. For several months we had been making contacts with people who had no families or friends and who were not being reached even by the churches. We therefore resolved that we would put on a Christmas meal for them.

Food was prepared and invitations given out. The response was overwhelming. So many wanted to come that a second day had to be arranged immediately. What a delightful time they had. Their faces glowed with joy as in the candlelight they sang the old familiar carols. For some it would be their only Christmas meal and the only occasion when they would be in the company of others over the festive period. This was not a church gathering; some had never been to church in their lives. The post-war materialism had seen to that. But now they were open and willing to listen to the story of God's love told to them by people who had already shown its reality by their actions.

Winter is usually the most difficult time for the elderly.

Fuel costs are high and for people on low fixed incomes this means economy to the point of deprivation. Each year there are numerous reports of deaths from hypothermia because the elderly are afraid to run up gas and electricity bills. But the cause can also be ignorance about steps to be taken to conserve body heat. Booklets giving helpful hints on how to keep warm in winter were produced by the local government and made available to the BCM. This provided us with an excellent opportunity to visit the elderly in their homes. What a reception our missionaries had! In addition to the cold, we found that the slippery condition of the pavements prevented old people from venturing out so that they were marooned in their homes. The visitors brought relief and cheer. All kinds of practical requests were made to them— collecting pensions, doing the shopping, household repairs and taking letters to the post. Whenever possible small gifts were taken to the elderly—a packet of tea, a bag of fruit or a tin of food. Knitted items such a scarfs, hats or even blankets were especially welcomed.

Such care is commonplace, always needed and undertaken by many. What special contribution could the city missionaries make which others would not? It was the spiritual dimension. Far from the concept that 'religion is the opium of the people', we found that humanistic materialism had drugged minds, preventing them from facing reality. In old age wealth and ambition lose their attraction. Sober thought of the life to come is more relevant, and the need to find forgiveness and hope more desirable. The missionaries did not need to apologise for reading the Bible to their clients and praying with them; they were welcomed, even requested, to do so. The Word of God never fails to give hope and comfort to those who seek it; the stories of Jesus are as spellbinding to the eighty-year-old as they are to the five-year-old, but much more satisfying. The practice of the presence of God which the Christian worker exercises is coveted by those who observe it. It is beyond price to all people who acquire it, and they can and do. Some, however, find it difficult or even resent the very idea.

One elderly gentleman made his wishes quite clear. 'I very much appreciate your visits,' he said, 'and I am grateful for the gifts you bring, and I want you to stay and talk to me, but I don't want you to read the Bible and pray with me.' He was a local man who had been active in the social life of the district all his life and was rather bitter against the God he did not know. 'I'm afraid I won't be able to visit you if I can't read the Bible and pray with you,' was the missionary's reply. 'This is what all our missionaries are required to do and we believe it will help you.' 'Well, I want you to keep coming so you had better read,' he conceded.

Some weeks later, I met the man in the street and he confided in me that he had now become a true Christian and was so glad for what he had learned from the missionary. He is one of many who have been helped by our Visiting Service for the Elderly, led by Diane Coles.

15

Mission Crusades

THE SIGHT OF THOUSANDS of people packed into a large football stadium to hear a gospel preacher is a most moving spectacle. The singing of a massed choir and powerful soloists creates an atmosphere of joyful expectation. When at the appeal hundreds of people of all ages leave their seats, file down the aisle and crowd around the rostrum to declare their faith, tears of joy are commonplace. One may be tempted to believe that this form of evangelism is the only effective means, and that all resources of finance, manpower and effort should be targeted there. There is no doubt that it is an important method of evangelism, but it is only part of the story. Often the evangelistic crusade simply acts as the climax of months or years of painstaking labour in prayer and personal witness.

During 1965, the year the BCM was founded, the evangelist Billy Graham held a crusade at Earls Court in London. A television link was made to relay the meetings to Bingley Hall, Birmingham, a place where Dr Moody and others had preached in years gone by. The new city mission threw its weight into the project, visiting districts untouched by local churches and inviting and providing transport for interested

people. Wesley Erpen, a young teenager, was one who went
forward at these meetings. As was mentioned above, later he
grew to be a fine Christian man and after training joined the
mission. He is now field leader responsible for overseeing
staff and training students.

Some years later Birmingham received two visits by
Arthur Blessitt, the American evangelist who toured the
world carrying a large wooden cross. Inevitably he attracted
much public attention, and he preached powerfully in the
open-air market area.

Large crowds gathered to hear him and many people were
truly converted. BCM workers again became deeply
involved both in counselling and in inviting people to the
meetings. Arthur once said that there should be people
witnessing on every street corner in the city. The mission
took up the challenge and during his second visit 120 volunteers were organised to preach and distribute literature on a
busy Saturday. Sixty thousand pieces of literature were given
away that day.

Arthur Blessitt was invited to Chelmsley Wood, a vast
new housing estate to the east of the city. The mission
organised a meeting in the park, the largest gathering ever
held in that area. On a beautiful sunny evening hundreds
attended this impromptu evangelistic crusade. The climax
came as people held hands to form enormous circles as they
sang God's praises. Enquirers were led from the field
through the subway into the nearby St Andrew's Church for
counselling. Among them was a young man with lots of
personal problems who had run away from home. He too
was later to join the mission, where he served for several
years.

In 1976 the BCM took the initiative in crusade evangelism.
East Birmingham is a sprawling area with a population of
about 300,000 people. Church attendance is extremely low.
Most of the houses were constructed after the war, when the
church was in decline, so few new churches were built, and

those that were had small congregations. As there is no proper centre to this district there are few public buildings. The most central position is Stechford, and for many years a fun fair has been held there at a point where several busy roads meet.

The BCM applied to use the plot of ground and invited evangelist Ron Spillards to bring a large tent for a special campaign. Twenty churches opted to join the crusade. The mission produced special literature and organised mass visitation and meetings in schools and clubs. Mission workers and volunteers cleared the ground, put up the tent, laid on water and electricity, erected seating and platforms, provided security and performed a hundred and one other tasks.

This tent campaign was a success. It provided an opportunity for mission workers and churches to bring people they had contacted and prayed for over the years to the meetings. The seed had been sown, now was the time for reaping. Among those who found Christ was the mother of a boy brought to the Lord by a mission worker, who later became an overseas missionary. The lady came to hear Doreen Irvine, the converted witch and authoress, who was one of the speakers. She turned to Christ and grew rapidly into a fine godly warrior who, until her death, prayed for us every day.

Mission England

One of the most effective evangelistic crusades in Britain took place in 1984 and was called Mission England. Birmingham was one of the venues, and its large Villa Park football stadium became a place of pilgrimage for tens of thousands. The weather had been unsettled but as soon as the first meeting was under way the sun shone from a cloudless sky. Over 3,000 people responded to Billy Graham's appeal on one evening alone. Those who attended will never forget the excitement, the joy, the singing, the clear preaching and the silent response. On a hill outside the stadium a huge TV screen was erected and thousands of people who could not get in watched in the overflow meeting.

In Birmingham, the Bull Ring was selected as the best site for a large portable building to serve as a ticket unit and information centre. Mission workers manned it each day. TV screens were erected and Billy Graham videos were shown to the passers-by. At the bookstalls placed there, large quantities of Christian literature were sold or given away. The missionaries were engaged in personal evangelism from morning to night. From time to time open-air meetings were held, sometimes with associate evangelists using public address equipment. BCM workers saw this whole crusade as a golden opportunity. Mission England and Billy Graham were news in the media. Thousands saw him interviewed on TV. Personal evangelism was needed to follow up the interest aroused. Here was a prime example of crusade and city mission evangelism working in perfect harmony.

BCM missionaries organised door-to-door visitation, inviting people to the central meetings. Many of the people contacted had been visited on previous occasions by district missionaries. Their hearts were already prepared by prayer. It came as no surprise when they responded to the invitation to give their lives to Christ.

After the crusade the BCM was in the forefront of caring for the new Christians, arranging home Bible studies and introducing them to local churches and wider experience of the Christian life. Some became involved in Christian service within the mission.

Challenge to the city

The following year, 1985, another special opportunity occurred for the BCM to become involved with crusade evangelism. The events are remarkable as an example of God's leading and an act of faith.

In April it first came to our attention that Sheffield, which had not been able to be involved with Mission England, was to be the venue of a Billy Graham crusade. The meetings were to be transmitted by satellite television to various places around the country. We learned that two sites had been chosen in Birmingham, one a church in Ward End and another a church in Handsworth. Nothing was planned for the city centre.

The evening following the receipt of this information was the night for the mission prayer meeting and the matter was prayed over. The next day, a Friday, a regular BCM staff meeting was held and it became clear that we should arrange a TV satellite mission in the centre of Birmingham if at all possible. Time was short and the likelihood of a large public auditorium being available was remote. To reduce what might have been a lengthy process we therefore asked ourselves which building we would most like to use. It was decided that the Odeon cinema in New Street would be best. Two thousand five hundred seats made it the largest auditorium in the city. There was a large screen and the seats were comfortable and arranged solely for viewing. Mark Lacey was despatched to see the Odeon manager. To our amazement he returned to say that although the cinema was heavily booked throughout the year, it was vacant for only the week of the Sheffield meeting. In faith we immediately booked it.

Only six weeks were left in which to acquire the equipment. We wanted the transmission to fill the very wide cinema screen and it was necessary to scour the country looking for the suitable lenses. In that time we also recruited stewards, counsellors, and follow-up personnel. Publicity material had to be acquired and distributed to the churches and the public. Tickets and posters were printed, newspapers and radio stations alerted.

One night I was awakened out of a sound sleep into a sudden realisation, which I can only think was the voice of the Lord. It was as if He said to me, 'You have rented the whole of the main cinema in Birmingham, use it.' 'What do you mean? How can I use it more?' 'Show the film *Jesus*,' was the startling reply. The next morning I rang International Films and was told that the 70mm version of the film *Jesus*, based on St Luke's Gospel, was available and that they would be happy to let me have it. Suddenly we were into another project, arranging publicity and notifying schools.

Each evening people thronged to the cinema, far more than had frequented the Odeon for years. Many were brought in off the main shopping streets by our missionaries and voluntary workers. Each afternoon crowds of schoolchildren watched the magnificent events in the life of Jesus and heard His words as recorded in the Gospel. Many of them came from Muslim and Hindu homes; others had never known the story of Jesus before. The children were invited to bring their parents to the cinema at night to hear Billy Graham. The evening meetings began with the trailer of the *Jesus* film inviting the audience to the film the next day. Outside the cinema, which is on Birmingham's main shopping street, I was astonished to see in large letters the billing, 'Tonight: Billy Graham . . . Tomorrow: Jesus'.

The result of this important evangelistic event run by the city mission was that 8,500 people attended the gospel meetings, 509 of whom responded to the invitation (6 per cent); of those who responded more than one third had no connection with any church. There were many stories of real conversion and years later many are strong in their faith. In addition, 1,220 people saw the film *Jesus*, of whom about 100 requested further help. A follow-up meeting called Live Link-Up was held in Carrs Lane centre. It was well attended and about a third of those present indicated that they had found Christ at the satellite meetings.

16

In The Bull Ring

'**D**ON'T YOU EVER bring anyone like that here again!' The angry words of the restaurant manageress rang in my ears.

As usual on a Tuesday afternoon we had been holding an open-air meeting. A crowd had gathered, mainly men. Even on a winter's day we often had forty men listening, many more if you include the passers-by. The crowd would always thicken if we were being heckled. They liked to listen to other people's arguments, especially if there was a touch of humour or pathos.

On this occasion a very dirty, ragged 'man of the road' had pushed his way to the front and begged for money. This was always an opportunity to bait the preacher. What would we do? The preacher was poor himself and had little money to spare and in all likelihood cash donated to such vagrants would subsidise their drinking habit. If, on the other hand, the peacher refused he would be accused of not caring and of unchristian behaviour.

'If you wait there until the end of the evening, Sir, I will buy you a cup of tea and something to eat.'

That seemed the best answer. No one could accuse me of

not caring, the audience was now on my side and I had gained another listener! The meeting finally ended and now I had to keep my promise. Nearby, I remembered, there was a tea bar where you could stand and eat cheaply. We went across and opened the door. To my horror the whole place had been altered. Instead of the former basic unfinished cafe there was a lovely modern restaurant with beautifully covered tables and chairs and attractively dressed waitresses.

Dirty Hands

It was too late, I couldn't back out, so we went in and sat at a table. I don't think my man had ever sat at a table before, much less been in a place like this. By now the smell of his unwashed body and clothing was getting to me. After a while I became conscious that the waitresses were steering clear of our table. Eventually I called across the room for one to serve us. She disappeared into the kitchen and reappeared with the washing-up lady in a white overall. It was she who took our order and later brought us the tea and sandwiches. Now he became awkward—there was not enough milk in his tea! I had to repeat the process of calling to a waitress who went out for the washing-up lady who, after enquiring what the fuss was about, went and fetched a jug of milk.

The vagrant's cup was now filled to the brim. Being an old alcoholic his hands trembled violently, spilling the tea. When he had finished his snack he beheld the scene. The beautiful white table-cloth was now a pool of mud on his side of the table. His hands had been so dirty that this was the result of the spilt tea. Moreover, I noticed that we were completely alone in our half of the restaurant, other customers having chosen to sit elsewhere or fled.

'Don't you ever bring any one like that here again,' the manageress called. But it was worth it!

The bad news

Drawing a crowd at the beginning of an open-air meeting is often a difficult task. In the Bull Ring I sometimes buy a newspaper from the man whose stand is near the old Woolworths store. Selecting headlines, I shout them from the rostrum to attract attention, and they form the introduction to the message.

One day I bought a copy of the *Evening Mail* and began to shout, 'This is a bad news paper.' From here and there in the paper I quoted items of 'bad news'. It is amazing how little good news is reported in the press, but that was not my point. I reiterated, 'This is a bad news paper.' At this point a smartly dressed young man began to heckle angrily. He was clearly upset by what was being said. I pointed out to him that the bad news was the result of man's sinfulness, violence and greed. The politicians and economists could hold out no hope. I turned to the Bible and said, 'This is a good news paper,' and explained that God had sent Jesus to free man from sin and bring hope to all.

The young man's angry questions and their answers caused a large crowd to gather. When other speakers took over I went to look for my opponent, but he had gone. 'Do you know who he is?' asked a team member. 'No, who is he?' I replied. 'He's a reporter for the *Evening Mail*. He thought you were attacking his paper by calling it a bad newspaper!'

Open-air preaching

The value of open-air preaching is that you meet people just where they are—on the street. Whether they stop and listen depends very much upon the preacher. Unless he has something to say and is interesting he will have no audience. He must also use language commonly in use, not religious technical words or jargon. Clichés are out. Nor is there room for doubters. The preacher must believe what he says, and say what he believes. His faith will be challenged. In church he speaks to a captive audience who are too polite to ask questions, challenge the arguments or just shout 'Rubbish!' Out of doors, however, all this happens, so he must know his Bible, think through his reasoning and have his wits about him. Sometimes there is a great deal of evil about, even violence, and earnest prayer is required before, after and during the meeting. In addition, it must be remembered that while in church the ratio may be twenty believers to one non-believer, in the open air it may be quite the other way .

It is always such a help when Christian friends stand with the preaching team to encourage them. Bert Arkinstall was such a man. At the time of his wife's death he became a Christian and after his retirement he made a regular practice of standing with us in the open air. He was never a preacher but could always give out tracts and witness personally.

Another regular supporter was Mr Loescher, an elderly farmer from near Walsall. In his later years he did not wish to negotiate the city traffic so he drove to Kingstanding in the suburbs and then took a bus to the city centre. He used to stand near the rostrum in an attitude of prayer. He didn't say much, but it was obvious that he was a godly man. He would stay to the end of the meeting, join us in prayer and offer to us words of advice and encouragement.

A similar person was an elderly Welshman who enjoyed occasions when there was heated debate. He was a bright, shining Christian, keen to witness for his Lord and whose very presence was an encouragement. Many years later I discovered that he was the father of Gilbert Hughes, a founder member of the new Swansea City Mission. Perhaps the old man's prayers had also found an answer in his native country.

In recent years open-air meetings have been led by our field leader, Wesley Erpen, or other members of staff, usually accompanied by a student team. They use modern methods such as a sketchboard or street drama. Earlier our main methods were question and answer or straight preaching.

A new recruit

There were odd occasions when help was not available for the Tuesday open-air meetings. One such occasion was when we had a tent mission elsewhere and all the staff were busy. I determined to go alone, hoping that some local Christians would turn up to help. No one came. I had taken the folding stand and put it in its usual place in the Bull Ring. Seeing no familiar faces I decided just to hand out literature to the passers-by. Still no friend appeared and I became embarrassed to think that market stallholders would have seen me bring the stand and not use it. Eventually I summoned up courage, and after prayer mounted the rostrum and began to preach. At first no one stopped but then one young man stood and listened. Having preached for a few minutes I felt I needed a break, and then noticed that the young man wore a 'Jesus Saves' badge. I stepped down, introduced myself to him, and tentatively asked if he would mind answering some questions from the stand. Rather timidly he agreed and nervously stepped on the rostrum. I asked him his name (I had never met him before), where he came from, why he wore his badge, how long he had been a Christian, how it happened and what Christ meant to him. His sincerity shone out as the unrehearsed dialogue continued. People stopped to listen to the stumbling words of the young man. Soon there was a good crowd and I was able to remount the stand and preach effectively to an attentive audience. When the meeting was over I questioned my young colleague and learned that this was the first time he had been asked to testify or speak in public.

The next week he was there again and was invited to share more. This continued each Tuesday for about six weeks, by which time he could not only testify confidently alone but also preach an effective message!

This method of learning has often been used since with students on our Inservice Training Course, and many a young preacher has been initiated into the techniques of addressing a crowd, and developed his art on the thronged pavements of the Bull Ring.

A waste of time?

Some would say that open-air preaching is outdated and fruitless. We have never found it to be so. The Lord's command is that we should go and preach, not that people should come and listen. Our archaic church buildings are seldom open. When they are, visitors have to contend with what is to them a strange culture of hymn singing and religious forms before they can get to hear what it is all about. Even then the messages are seldom relevant to their situations and there is little opportunity for them to ask questions. The church is often an exclusive club into which the visitor finds it hard to become integrated. Church members are different from the non-Christian by their dress, their behaviour and language. They speak in clichés and use a jargon foreign to the outsider. Every chorus is a new one to be learned, and finding one's way around the Bible or Prayer Book is an ordeal.

Not so in the open air. There all are equal. No frills are necessary or expected. The passer-by is on his own ground. If anything, it is the churchgoer who is the visitor. His faith will be challenged and he will be asked to explain it in simple, everyday language. Nor will the end of the meeting be the end of the matter. Long afterwards little groups will be seen debating the issues, and here and there someone prays and does business with God.

No such meeting is effective without personal counselling for enquirers and the prayerful passing on of appropriate Christian literature. This work is often fruitful, never a waste of time.

Once I was accused by an onlooker of wasting my time.

'What makes you say that?' I asked. 'I've been watching and listening to you preaching for an hour,' he said, 'but I haven't seen anyone converted yet.' 'Then you are in a serious situation,' I retorted. Pointing to a road sign warning of a hazard ahead because of road works I said, 'You see that sign? If it wasn't there and someone ran into a hole in the road there would be a row. People must be warned of danger ahead.' I explained that besides converting people it was the preacher's responsibility to warn his hearers of the dangers of neglecting their spiritual welfare or rejecting Christ. Then I went on to say to him, 'In case I may have been wasting my time, let me make sure you know the importance of this opportunity you have had to hear the gospel and the danger of neglecting it.' He was then gently but firmly warned and urged to receive Christ as his Saviour, being mindful that St Paul told the Ephesians to remember that he never stopped warning each of them night and day with tears (Acts 20:31).

The invitation

God moves in a mysterious way His wonders to perform, says the hymnwriter, and nowhere is this more true than in the work of converting the sinner. Many times we have sensed the presence of the Spirit of God in the busy market area called the Bull Ring. It is almost as if the rowdy clamours of the market traders, and even the city traffic is hushed as Jesus Himself draws near. He promised that if He was lifted up He would draw all men to Him, and He does. There is something very special about a simple but graphic portrayal of the person of Jesus Christ. His wisdom is irrefutable, His character unassailable, His life irreproachable and His death inimitable. Always there is a division among people because of Him. There is no neutral ground—we choose Him or reject Him. Many, counting the cost, like the rich young man in the Bible, turn away sadly. But there are always others who say in their hearts, 'To whom else shall we go? You have the words of eternal life.'

The invitation is given after preaching, but here we must exercise great care. Is it reasonable that a person bent on pleasure or business should be stopped in the street, and after hearing one short presentation of Christ, be expected to decide to change his whole style of living? It does happen that way sometimes, but it is more likely that that person begins a process of inquiry which will take time and further consideration before the instant of life-changing decision arrives. Nevertheless, it is an awesome moment when such a random gathering of people in the street pauses in silence to pray. The prayer is deliberate, slow and clear. Each short statement is followed by a pause to allow the hearers time to make it their own. Then finally there is an impassioned intercession for each person present and the families they represent.

To conclude the meeting the preacher offers a portion of the Bible or a New Testament, with other helpful literature, insisting that it should be taken only by those who have earnestly prayed the prayer and that they promise they will read the book all the way through.

Rooms to let?

Rupert Abbott had moved into a little house in Chartist Road to become a missionary in the mainly Muslim district of Saltley. Just round the corner, on the main road, was a butcher's shop. Soon he discovered that the young shop-keeper was a Christian. One day when he was there to buy some meat Rupert's little boy asked to go to the toilet. Stan Davis, the butcher, said they could use the one upstairs. While up there the missionary noticed that the rooms were empty and unused. A discussion ensued, resulting in the arrangement that the apartment be turned into an office and reception area for missionary work. It needed some alterations, decorating and furnishing.

When the work was completed, I, as mission director, was invited to visit the place. Access was through the butcher's shop. With a simple greeting to Stan Davis, who was serving a customer, I went upstairs, but when I came down he confronted me. 'So you are Mr Orton' he said, 'I had heard of you from Rupert but did not realise who you were.'

He then told me the story of how he used to work in the wholesale meat market in the city and how he used to pass by the Bull Ring open-air meeting. One day he had stopped to listen and been convicted by the message which he had heard. He was one of those who went forward to receive a New Testament. Since then he had not only read it but had become a committed Christian, active in a local church. We had not met again until that day when he recognised me as the preacher.

Since then Stan and his wife have been faithful supporters and prayer partners of the BCM. He has been training for the ministry and at the time of writing is a part-time worker in the BCM hostel.

A birthday thank you

The meeting had just ended and we were about to pack up our belongings when a young Birmingham man in his twenties stepped forward. He had a package in his hand and said, 'I would like you to accept this as a gift.'

Not recognising him I thanked him but asked why he was giving it to me.

'Today is my first birthday as a Christian,' he replied. 'I received Christ as my Saviour here in the Bull Ring a year ago. This is my way of saying thank you to you and to God for all that He has done for me.'

He went on to tell me how he was now an active member of a church in Selly Oak. When I opened the parcel I found that it contained a new cassette tape recorder. BCM workers soon put the gift to good use, and on one occasion recorded an open-air meeting in progress.

A life revolutionised

Recently I attended a prayer meeting for OM Leaders in London. After I had been speaking, a leader who had just returned from India stepped forward to tell me how he used to attend the Bull Ring open-air meetings. Then an atheist he used to heckle us violently. Apparently he, too, had gone forward to receive a Gospel of St John and promised to read it. Some time later he had done so, and through it he had been brought to Christ, his life had been revolutionised and later he had become a missionary.

Converted and cured

We shall never know in this life the true results of open-air preaching in a city centre. Many of our listeners are only visiting or passing through the city. This was the case of a fellow from Scunthorpe. Nothing was known to us about this man until we were sent a cutting from a Scunthorpe local newspaper. It was the story of a drug addict who had become a Christian and been cured of his addiction. In it, he said that he had been travelling by train and needed to change at New Street, Birmingham. As he had time to spare before his next connection he decided to go for a walk around the city. He came across the Bull Ring where members of the Birmingham City Mission were preaching. This had challenged him so deeply that it had led to his conversion.

The paper man

The meetings are frequently disturbed by angry opponents. We have had missiles thrown at us, been physically attacked, sworn at, slandered and pulled from the stand. Our attackers have mainly been drunks or drug addicts. Some have had a hatred of religion because of some deep hurt in their own lives. We have been harangued by Marxists, Jehovah's Witnesses, IRA supporters, fanatical Muslims and many others. Satan uses many means but sometimes oversteps himself.

A certain newspaper seller used to cause us many problems. If he saw that we had an attentive crowd he would make it his business to try to sell his newspapers among them, calling out loudly. When anyone sought to quieten him he would blaspheme and accuse us of all manner of evil.

One wintry day we were preaching as usual, but with few hearers. The newspaper seller had his arms full of papers and was passing by, not bothering us on this occasion. Suddenly a strong gust of wind caught the papers and blew them out of his arms and across the street. Seeing the poor man's dilemma, I left the stand and ran to help him. Together we collected the papers and helped him on his way. This man was never a nuisance to us again. Sometimes he would even stop and listen to the gospel. Then one day he asked to speak to me. He told me that he had to go to hospital for a serious operation and asked me to pray for him. There and then we prayed, the paper man and the preacher. When we finished he had tears in his eyes. I never saw him again.

17

What Is Special About City Missions?

D AVID NASMITH'S FIRST CITY MISSION in Glasgow bridged the gap between churches of different denominations. This was a new idea. The early nineteenth century was a time when churchmen held dearly to their doctrines and methods. There were deep divisions between them. Nasmith realised that the unchurched, especially the poor, were neglected and could be reached only by the concerted effort of united Christians willing to put their differences behind them. From that time city missions have led the way for effective co-operation in Christian ministry.

The Birmingham City Mission recognised the need for an interdenominational position from the beginning. The first committee members and supporters were drawn from a wide spectrum of denominational affiliations. At its inaugural meeting representatives from over fifty churches of most denominations, and none, attended. The trend has continued, so that on its various advisory councils and committees there are clergymen, pastors and leaders from many different churches.

One of the first tasks of the founding committee was to

draw up a list of beliefs which they felt most Christians have in common. This formed the basis of faith and was later incorporated into the mission's trust deed. The objective and practices of the mission were also included, besides procedural matters. When the deed was completed under the careful supervision of a noted Christian solicitor, it was signed and witnessed and then submitted to the Charity Commissioners for registration.

Although the deed allows no compromise regarding the essential Christian message and the Lordship of Christ, it makes no prohibition regarding methods of government or teachings not essential to salvation. Concerning controversial matters, the mission tries to keep a middle-of-the-road position. The intention is that nothing should be allowed to hinder the proclamation of the Word of God to those who have not heard, and the care of the needy, whoever they may be.

Clear definition of the purposes and scope of the mission and the establishment of a legally constituted trust were considered vital. Only such a trust could be responsible for funds donated or receive legacies or claim tax relief. Rules were also necessary regarding the way money would be spent and administered. Officers were appointed and auditors engaged. It was recognised that the mission must be accountable to its supporters for all funds and properties from whatever source received. Annual audited accounts have always been made public. This is essential if money is to be obtained from government departments or charitable trusts, but was considered good practice in any event.

In drawing up the constitution the founders tried to be forward-looking and not to make restrictions which would later inhibit the operations of their successors. That area known as the Midlands of England was defined as its territory, but no restrictions were placed on involvement in worldwide mission. Though couched in legal language the intentions were patent—that the society exists to preach the gospel to all, especially those outside the normal reach of the churches, and to provide a practical demonstration of the love of God by caring for the needy.

Church and mission

Surely it is the work of the local church to reach the neighbourhood with the gospel? Doesn't the para-church organisation weaken the local church? Do we really need to provide for the needy in these days of the welfare state? Aren't city missions out of date? These are some of the questions we are continually asked. The answer to the first question is, yes, it is the work of the local church. But how many are able to fulfil the responsibility?

Some years ago I remember making contact in the city with a couple involved with Jehovah's Witnesses. They invited me to their home in the suburbs. There they told me that they had had no religious background but they often talked together about God. Because there were so many different churches they were reluctant to choose one to attend, so they decided to wait for someone to call on them. After many months the only people who called were the JWs. How sad it was, for I know that just a couple of hundred yards away is a fine evangelical church where I have been invited to preach several times.

How often this is the case. If this can happen within the vicinity of an active church, how often must it be that people do not hear the truth about Jesus in less privileged areas?

Of course, it remains the local church's duty to reach its own neighbourhood. The city mission should never be seen as competitor in this. Rather, it is an agent for help to the local fellowship. Missionaries are well trained and experienced evangelists, willing to lead and train ordinary church members to win others.

Many churches in Birmingham have had mission teams working with them, bringing inspiration and encouragement to their members. Sometimes series of meetings are held in which training is given in various forms of evangelism suitable for the district. These conclude with the missionaries taking the members on door-to-door visitation, to open-air meetings or on children's missions. Such activities certainly strengthen, not weaken, the local church.

Regarding the matter of the welfare state providing for the needy, it should be borne in mind that it is a Christian's duty to clothe the naked, feed the hungry, visit the sick and those in prison. These were the criteria on which judgement hinged in Christ's parable of The Sheep and The Goats. That the government does so much does not do away with this responsibility. And there are huge gaps in the welfare system. Traditionally the church provided care for the poor, the sick and the homeless. Many state institutions were originally founded and run by the church. After years of state involvement the voluntary sector, in which the church has a large share, is being asked to play a much more active role. Local churches, however, are not necessarily equipped to meet the need, but the missions they support may be able to. Some churches do become involved in caring for the wider community, but all too often the needs require specialist attention. Here the mission is well placed to receive referrals from the local vicar or church leader. Experienced mission workers can tell the difference between the genuinely needy person and con men. The mission provides neutral ground for counselling and treatment. It has the facilities for providing shelter, food and clothing and for dealing with the alcoholic and the drug abuser. A referral network of specialist agencies is readily available, and the good reputation of an established mission enhances the chances of its clients to gain housing or financial benefits.

Co-operation between church and mission is not only mutually beneficial, but is in the best interest of all they seek to serve. City missions become a clearing house for surplus goods, information and manpower. For the church the mission becomes 'our mission'—a practical, observable and measurable involvement in care and outreach to a world in which they are strangers.

In these days when existing cities are growing in size and new cities are being developed it seems obvious that city missions will be needed more than ever. If they are to succeed they must move with the times and address themselves to the needs of the day, using modern techniques to meet them. However, the message is the same. The gospel is still the power of God for the salvation of everyone who believes.

Mission personnel are, of course, church members themselves. No mission would accept on to its staff anyone who was not only a believer but also actively involved in his own church life. Any new applicant for mission service must be recommended by his church as a person of Christian character. Mission staff who join from another area are expected to attend a church in their new locality.

Work within the mission is no substitute for local church life and missionaries are encouraged not only to participate in its worship but also accept its discipline. We must respect the ministry of others. Although we may be convinced of the importance of our work, we realise that it is only part of the overall work of God. This is not only desirable but economical and practical.

From its beginning the BCM has been grateful for the co-operation of Scripture Union, Open Air Mission, Child Evangelism Fellowship, Scripture Gift Mission, Christian Literature Crusade, The Bible Society and many other Christian organisations. Speakers and lecturers are invited from other missions at home and overseas. Our first Inservice Training student was referred by the Worldwide Evangelisation Crusade, and since then students have come from and been referred to various Bible Colleges and societies. City missions are local missionary societies in fellowship with the work of God everywhere.

In Britain there are no official connections between the

individual city missions. Historically they were mainly founded by Nasmith but each evolved in its own way. They differ in legal constitution, administration and methods of funding. Basically they are Protestant, evangelical and inter-denominational. One is a limited company, another is a registered denomination, one is strongly linked with the Presbyterian Church. The European city missions are mainly connected with the Lutheran Church.

Prayer and faith

As we have seen, the new Birmingham City Mission chose to be interdenominational and also to be a faith mission. This needs clarifying, for it is not meant to imply that other missions are not missions of faith. But the main emphasis at the BCM was one of prayer and trust in God for the supply of its needs. No public appeals were to be made for funding its evangelism.

During the years there has been some modification in that a distinction has been made between the mission's spiritual work and its caring activities. Believing that most social needs are created by the society we live in, the mission felt that it was right to appeal to the government and charitable trusts to meet those needs. For the spiritual work, including the salaries of the missionaries, there would be total dependence upon God through prayer.

Prayer is the Christian lifeline. It is also that discipline whereby God's people discover the will of God. By His response or lack of response He is seen to act as Head of His church and therefore to be in control. Without going into detail at this point, it has been made abundantly clear to us that this is the way the BCM should work. Budgeting has been made in the light of this. The question is always 'Are you sure we are in the will of God?' If so, then we can go ahead and plan the project, trusting that when the funds are needed He will supply.

When times of testing have come, and there have been

many, a careful review is necessary to see if we are still in the will of God. There are times when a project is no longer needed.

A leader of another city mission was sharing a particular problem. For several years they had been saving up to buy a special vehicle to be used as a mobile soup kitchen, but funds had been so slow in coming in that the price of the van was rising faster than the income. At that rate they would never purchase one. I explained how we operated in the BCM and asked him if they were sure it was God's will that they should buy the vehicle. When he said they had no doubts about it, I suggested that they should just go ahead and order one and trust the Lord to supply.

A few weeks later I was invited to their city to speak at a service of dedication of the new, fully equipped mobile unit, which had been completely paid for. God is faithful to His promises.

Planting, supporting and communicating

Missionaries in some city missions are pastors of churches. In fact some mission halls are really chapels in which all the usual religious services are held and are conducted by the missionary. In the BCM we have not felt that this should be our policy. Our task is to proclaim the gospel to those who would not otherwise hear, to reach the unreached for Christ. For this we need the support of all the Christian churches. We felt that it would be unreasonable for these churches to be expected to support other churches, run by the mission, especially if their doctrines and practices differed from their own. The matter of ordination is also controversial. Our missionaries are commissioned as evangelists, not pastors or ministers. Some, of course, become very able preachers and receive invitations to become pastors or train for the ministry. They are free to do so, but must leave the mission. We do not consider such a change in ministry to be a kind of promotion to something better. Rather, we feel that there is no higher calling than that in which we are engaged, but that of course each one of us must fulfil his own ministry.

There are times when it may appear that we do not act consistently with these principles. Several BCM missionaries are responsible for leading local fellowships. Three reasons may be given for this. First, the mission is committed to starting new churches in areas such as housing estates where no church exists. This is a church-planting situation and the missionary acts as leader only until the church decides on which form of government or denomination it wishes to adopt. Then another leader will be appointed and the city missionary moves on.

Second, the mission is committed to keeping open churches which are in danger of closing. Many inner city churches become weakened because of redevelopment and population changes. Typically, a few elderly people are left after the young people have moved into the suburbs. But the district is as heavily populated as ever, usually by Asian or other foreign residents and by poorer non-churchgoers who need much support. Rather than see such churches close, BCM missionaries go and take on leadership. We prefer to send small teams. These help with the running of the church. If the church develops and grows then the same church-planting policy we have already mentioned applies. If not, we do not consider the work to be a church but rather a mission station for evangelistic outreach.

Third, there are some missionaries who belong to churches which do not employ full-time pastors and are invited to act as such in their own time. This is allowed, as it would be if they were asked to become deacons or Sunday school teachers, but it is done in the worker's own time. He is not paid by the BCM to do the work and his commitment to the BCM takes precedence.

Most misunderstandings between the church and the mission are due to difficulties in communication. Denominational churches naturally communicate best between themselves and it is not easy for outsiders to penetrate the system. In any case, there is a constant change of leaders and officers in the church, and of course changes of address create problems of communication.

The BCM tries to deal with this by constantly updating its records on computer, but we must have the information first! Monthly newsletters are sent to all prayer partners. A quarterly magazine is sent to all others on the mailing lists. The mission provides pulpit speakers for all sorts of churches and fellowships. Deputation meetings are conducted by missionaries whenever they are invited. Mission students are placed in churches which request them. Each year an open day is organised to which the Christian public is invited to see for itself the mission properties and meet the mission workers in their various localities. The day ends with a public meeting for praise, worship, testimony and the ministry of God's Word.

The Annual General Meeting of the BCM is the most important part of the attempt to have good communication with the local churches. Every effort is made by personal invitations, letters, the press and local radio to bring together a fully representative body to the central gathering. A full report is made of all the mission's activities which is not only presented at the meeting but also published and circulated around the country.

At this meeting new staff and students are also introduced. Regular staff make their own reports and the accounts of the mission are made public. The closing speaker is usually an able, experienced Christian worker. Each year the speaker is chosen from a different denomination or organisation. Other city missions are represented but mainly the chief guest is a leader of a local Birmingham church. Then the city mission is not seen as a rival in the city. Instead, the churches can all say that the BCM is *our* mission.

18

Here And Now

TRUTH IS STRANGER than fiction, it is said. Certainly it is a great deal more interesting. Nowhere is this more so than in the story of the Christian church. After all, the 'church' is just a word for a vast number of individuals. Their personal stories of conversion, achievements, suffering and martyrdom would satisfy the voracious appetites of the tabloid press in any age.

When I first became a Christian I had a real hunger for such human stories. At the age of seventeen I waded through Mrs Howard Taylor's biography of the founder of the China Inland Mission, *Hudson Taylor in Early Years*. Someone gave me the published journals of David Livingstone which I read avidly, and I revelled in the life of George Muller of Bristol. The stories of William Carey of India, David Jones of Madagascar, Adoniram Judson of Burma and many others never failed to captivate my imagination.

The problem was that whenever I heard of the wonderful works of God they either happened a long way away, or a long time ago. Little seemed to be happening here and now. Of course it never occurred to me that such a present, immediate experience of God at work could be mine personally. Like many other things in life, this only happened to other people.

How wrong I was is surely demonstrated by the contents of this book. Time and time again we have found ourselves caught up in the doings of God. He is working today, and in the unattractive greyness of the urban culture exemplified by Birmingham. Since the simple beginnings in November 1965 we have often been called on to work hard and make great efforts of faith, but more frequently to stand still and see God at work. He is quite capable of doing without our help, but He chooses to use ordinary weak and foolish people to fulfil His purposes of grace.

It is easier to describe what is 'here' than what is 'now', because the 'now' of today is history tomorrow. However we shall attempt to do so by defining 'now' as the 1990s, twenty-five years after the BCM started.

Reaching the unreached

Today the needs of this city are greater that ever. Our current Annual Report talks of the unlovely side Birmingham has, in common with many other cities.

> The crime rate continues to climb. Attacks upon the weak and defenceless are on the increase. So is drunkenness, drug addiction and sexually transmitted disease. The old are neglected, the children abused and the poor exploited. Muggers and rapists stalk the unwary. Many, especially the elderly, live in fear. Spiritually too there is decline....

To fulfil the main objectives of the city mission the work of evangelism occupies chief place. Open-air meetings for preaching the gospel take place several times a week in various locations. Modern methods are used to convey the message and free literature is distributed. Here and there people's lives are being changed as they respond to the message.

Door-to-door visitation takes place weekly in sixteen dis-

tricts. Thousands of *Messenger* papers are delivered by this
means. About 250 Bible study meetings are held weekly in
homes contacted through visitation. One church reports that
about thirty people have joined because of the ministry.
Daily stories are told of needy people being contacted and
helped practically—the bereaved are comforted, the bro-
ken-hearted are healed and the poor have the good news
preached to them.

Several of our missionaries are recognised hospital chap-
lains who have wards allocated to them. They are appreciated by staff and patients because the missionary is free to be
a link between the sick person and his home. Sometimes the
family needs the help which only the mission can give.

Visitation of the elderly is a special service to shut-in
isolated people otherwise deprived of family and friends.
Though this is largely a caring service providing all kinds of
help and liaising with statutory and voluntary agencies, it
provides a unique spiritual ministry to the unchurched. Community meals are provided for senior citizens, but always
followed with a suitable devotional time. This is particulary
welcomed at Christmas. In the summer, outings to the country are much appreciated by these people.

Young people are regularly reached by the mission's
Youth and Schools Department. Many schools are visited
regularly by the missionaries, who conduct assemblies and
give lessons on issues of current importance. A Christian
view is presented and healthy discussion encouraged. Some
schools hold Christian Union meetings in the lunch hour or
weekend houseparties, where our workers can be more direct in leading the young to Christ. The BCM holds its own
camps in the summer, and in the latest report thirty-six
youngsters are said to have made professions of faith.

Mission centres

The BCM's trust deed states that it is committed to supporting churches in danger of closing. Redevelopment of the

inner city creates changes in the population. Young families connected with a church are often rehoused in the suburbs, leaving a declining elderly congregation. The district around the church is repopulated with immigrants from overseas, single-parent or less able families, who are usually poor and disadvantaged. Such people are not naturally churchgoers and present a challenge to evangelism.

Cromwell Hall in Winson Green is one such case. It is now a BCM Trust property, though the services continue on the same lines as they did under the former administration. Paul Amos, a BCM missionary, has moved into the neighbourhood with his wife and child. Another staff member and two students assist him in visitation, outreach and the development of the hall as an evangelistic and caring centre.

Hodge Hill Gospel Church is another centre situated on the east side of the city. Jeremy Andrews and his wife and children have moved there to be responsible for the work which may otherwise have closed. Besides special activities for the elderly they have started a thriving work among the mothers and toddlers.

Firs Chapel, Quinton, is also the mission's responsibility. The authorities have stated that the area around the chapel is the most socially deprived district in Birmingham. Terry Head, a BCM staff worker, has been there for many years and has recently been joined by Ian Richardson and his wife and child. The work is small but growing.

Fatherless Barn Church and Kingshurst Evangelical Church are not mission properties but are both in areas of great need and have had the services of mission staff for many years. Today the former is led by Wesley Erpen, our field leader, who lives there with his wife and children. Two BCM students work alongside the church at Kingshurst under the supervision of Paul Olise, who lives and works with his family at the nearby Chelmsley Wood estate. Paul, who came to England from Western Africa, worked for several years in the multi-racial area of Handsworth before taking up his present appointment. Chelmsley Wood is a Birmingham housing estate built in the early seventies, with a population of 60,000 people.

Bartley Green Gospel Hall is the most recent addition to the mission's responsibilities. The area on the west of the city was once a small village but is now surrounded by new houses and flats. As no staff member is yet available, two BCM students are visiting the districts and using the chapel for their base.

The Castle Vale Fellowship, originally started by BCM workers, is now a fully independent church. Nevertheless, strong ties remain and Ian and Judie Hare and their children moved to the district five years ago and do valiant work in the district. At present Ian is also the evangelistic leader of the student team. Plans are at an advanced stage for opening a mission care shop on the estate. It is expected that the BCM warehouse will also be situated there. The fellowship continues to grow—people are converted and baptised necessitating extensions to the building.

Saltley has seen some of the most exciting work done by the mission. Rupert and Janet Abbott have lived there with their children for many years, working first with an office above the butcher's shop and more recently from rooms of the Saltley Methodist Church in the busy shopping area of Alum Rock. Besides building up strong community relations with the mainly Muslim population, they have developed a vital role as district missionaries related to most of the churches of various denominations. Both Rupert and Janet speak the Urdu language and communicate freely with Pakistani neighbours, having entrance into many of their homes. They receive invitations to several schools in the district, most of which have mainly Asian children. Friendship evangelism adapted to the local culture is engaged in daily.

In addition to the districts where staff missionaries live and work, BCM students are also working alongside

churches in Bearwood, Edgbaston, Lea Hall, South Yard-
ley, Spring Hill and Stechford.

The mission's headquarters in Arden Road, Acocks
Green, has been used for evangelism on various occasions.
Currently it is the centre for the work among the elderly, and
also runs a mothers and toddlers club. The busy offices are
often used for counselling people who call in person or by
phone. Evangelistic correspondence is also undertaken and
Scriptures and booklets sent by post.

Caring hands

People are not only spirits, and the role of the city mission
must be to minister to the whole person. His physical needs
must be met on equal terms, and often these must come first.
To this end thousands of meals are prepared for needy
people in our hostel, soup kitchen, bus project, youth camps
and lunch clubs for the elderly. Many other services are daily
being provided by the BCM.

The hostel in Granville Street is well staffed, well equipped, clean and warm and much appreciated by residents
and transient homeless people. During the past year 380
people were accommodated. Ninety-eight were women and
girls. Of those admitted, 50 per cent stayed less than a week,
20 per cent between a week and a month and 20 per cent up
to six months. Eighteen men have been there for a year or
more. The chief cause of their homelessness is alcohol and
drug abuse, followed by mental illness, crime, marriage and
family breakdown, and physical and emotional inadequacy.

Each person being admitted is first fed, then provided
with soap and a towel and plenty of warm water for a bath or
shower. He or she is given clean underclothes and other
garments if necessary, and then allocated a bed with freshly
laundered sheets. Next day he is helped to sort out his
financial and other problems with the local Social Security
office. During his stay he is able to sit in the comfortable
lounge, watch TV, play games or learn new skills in the

basement workshop. Besides general care, the hostel staff, supported by willing volunteers provide an excellent Christmas for the homeless. Outings recently arranged have been to Derbyshire, Weston-Super-Mare, Warwickshire, Malvern and the Cotswolds.

The house in Acocks Green which was bought to accommodate BCM students has now been converted into a hostel for homeless women. It has been refurbished with a beautiful kitchen and two modern bathrooms. Thirteen women can be cared for in pleasant secure surroundings. Female staff have been engaged so that women from the emergency shelter in Granville Street city centre unit can be given further help and rehabilitation.

Major changes in BCM city centre work took place in 1989. No. 36 Bromsgrove Street, which had become so dear to many of us, had at last to be vacated due to redevelopment. It has now disappeared and in its place the new modern China Town is being constructed. We cannot complain—our centre was originally let to us for six months but that period was extended to twenty years!

The soup kitchen has been transferred to Spring Hill. Premises are being rented from the city council but soon the work will be transferred to the crypt of St Peter's Church nearby. The soup kitchen supplies food and clothing for desperately needy men and women. Between twenty and thirty attend during the evenings.

In addition, the centre doubles as a warehouse for furniture, equipment and clothing. These items are sorted, renovated and distributed. Former residents of our hostel who move into rooms provided by the city council are given beds, cookers and other furniture. Bob George, assisted by volunteers, is full time in the work and a large mission van is used for collection and deliveries. Bob came from a difficult home situation which made him an aggressive, bitter teenager. After serving as a professional soldier he had a wonderful conversion experience. Such a history has made him able to identify with some of the most needy people. While he is able to give practical help he is also able to share his faith.

A smart shop painted in the mission colours of blue and white and situated on the busy outer circle bus route serves as our present charity shop, or Care Shop as it is called. Terry Head, a former merchant seaman, who was drunken and violent before his conversion, now attends to the needs of poorer people requiring clothing and other necessities of life. Above the shop is a fine spacious apartment used to accommodate four BCM students.

Birmingham hosts an annual Super Prix road race which is a gala occasion attracting many thousands of people. The race begins in Bristol Street, where today the mission has its bookshop and evangelistic centre. It lies just a few hundred yards from the old familiar centre in the next street, but the new shop is modern, well equipped and stocked with a wide range of Bibles and Christian books. A video library is well used by Christian workers from around the Midlands.

Above the shop is a large room used by the missionaries to prepare for their open-air meetings and other evangelistic outreach in the city centre. Workers can easily walk from there to the Bull Ring and return with needy people for counselling.

Two other rooms serve as a counselling room and offices for mission leaders. In the basement a large storeroom acts as a reception centre for goods donated to the mission.

The building is in the heart of the city and serves as a busy focal point for mission activities of all kinds. Almost £14,000 worth of books were sold to the general public during the past year. At Christmas good sales were made at bookstalls in the High Street and the Bull Ring. Books have also been sold at numerous summer carnivals, exhibitions and home book parties.

'Have you thought about buying a double-decker bus?' The question was asked in a letter from a brother who said he was praying about the replacement of 36 Bromsgrove

Street. Each time he prayed he had had a vision of a bus and felt the Lord was saying something to us. I'm afraid I was rather dismissive as I couldn't imagine us owning a bus. The letter was put in a file pending an answer.

One morning Rupert Abbott asked me if I had thought about buying a bus for our work among the homeless. As he knew nothing about the letter I could only conclude that the Lord was speaking to us. Enquiries were made, plans drawn up and eventually we were able to buy a secondhand bus from Derby. The former owners did all the work of converting it to our use, fitting it out as a modern unit and painting on it the BCM sign of the Outstretched Hands in the familiar blue and white colours.

Today the bus is paid for and being used as a mobile soup kitchen in the evenings, a mobile charity shop, exhibition unit and bookshop in the daytime. It is a familiar sight around the city and plays a significant part in reaching out to proclaim the gospel and to care for the needy.

To run the mission with its more than thirty staff, fourteen full-time students and about forty volunteers, a great deal of support is needed. Audited accounts for the year ended 31 March 1990 show a total turnover of £424,486, divided almost equally between the hostel fund and the general fund. The latter depends almost entirely on freewill donations which come in answer to prayer and faith. The mission's total assets are recorded as £177,015.

These figures represent many transactions and a great deal of correspondence and administration. This is conducted from our Acocks Green headquarters using modern equipment. Each member of the office staff is a committed Christian who feels privileged to serve the Lord in this way.

Just a few days before writing this we held a meeting and provided a meal for people who had been attending the Spring Hill soup kitchen. One man asked to speak to me privately. He was obviously a bright Christian and we prayed together. Then he told me his story of how he used to be an alcoholic and lived rough. He attributes his conversion to the mission's patient caring work and also its evangelistic out-reach. How lovely it was to hear his simple prayer from his heart for the mission. How wonderful to know that our labour has not been in vain.

19

The Wider Scene

CITIES CHANGE. Glasgow, once noted for the dark poverty of the Gorbals tenements, has recently been voted European City of Culture. Liverpool has recovered from its troubles in Toxteth to become renowned as a garden city. The new city of Milton Keynes has been born. On the world scene urbanisation is growing at an incredible rate.

David Nasmith had little idea of how his city missions would become such agents of change. For more than a century and a half they have been changing men and helping to change society. His first mission was in Glasgow, then Dublin. Both these societies still exist, though others which he founded no longer do.

North America

In 1990 a new mission was started in New Orleans, USA. This was sponsored by the International Union of Gospel Missions, an association of rescue missions mainly in North America. It is strange that we have records to show that Nasmith also visited New Orleans to start a city mission in 1831. He visited America and Canada, founding missions in

New York, Boston, Philadelphia and other cities. Usually he collected a group of interested people, talked about the nature of the work, challenged them to start and appointed a committee and offices. Then he moved on. It is unclear whether any of these missions have survived, but the idea certainly has because the IUGM consists of almost 300 missions engaged in similar work today.

Each year the IUGM holds a Convention. In 1987 it was held in Syracuse, New York, and attended by over 300 delegates. It was the occasion of the one hundredth anniversary of the Syracuse City Mission. The scale and scope of its work is beyond anything in Britain. Although that mission has less of an evangelistic emphasis, it was refreshing to meet so many people whose lives had been reclaimed from alcoholism, drug addiction and other vices. Thousands of people were present at the closing banquet held in the university sports arena. Special video messages were presented from the USA President, Ronald Reagan, and the evangelist, Dr Billy Graham. The speaker was the world renowned writer, Joni Erikson Tada.

The missions in North America have a long record of rescuing thousands of men and women from sin and influencing their country for good. Some mission leaders are themselves evidence; for example, the converted drunk Jerry Dunn, whose book *God is for the Alcoholic* is in demand worldwide. IUGM links up these missions, which vary in size and operations. It runs training programmes and district conferences, sets standards of performance, publishes specialist manuals, and promotes new missions.

Australia

Australia's bicentenary celebrations in 1988 provided an opportunity for an International Convention of City Missions to be held in Sydney. Delegates were shown around some of the thirty-five centres of the Sydney City Mission, one of the largest in the world. Missionbeat street patrol is a service with four 24-hour radio-controlled vans, which that year made over 22,000 pick-ups of homeless people. Over 10,000 distressed people received help over the mission's Startover counselling telephone service. Their Family Welfare Service provided 30,000 families on the poverty line with food, clothing and counselling. Hundreds of unemployed people received job training, and many alcoholic, drug-dependent men and women and young people received shelter, medical attention and care through the work of Sydney City Mission.

The Melbourne City Mission has, adjoining its headquarters, a beautiful hospice caring for fifty terminally ill patients. Surrounded by acres of landscaped gardens is the mission's modern purpose-built village for the elderly. Devoted godly Christians run these projects, where an atmosphere of the love of God pervades.

In Launceston, Tasmania, there is a small but fine city mission, founded in 1854. Outreach in the town is done in conjunction with students from the local WEC Bible College. They have a 'Mobile Mission' double-decker bus, a drive-in market and three opportunity shops.

The oldest city mission in the southern hemisphere is in Hobart, Tasmania. For 188 years the gospel has been preached and the needy cared for in this most beautiful part of the world.

Other Australian missions are in Adelaide, Newcastle, Brisbane, Wollongong and elsewhere. There are also city missions in New Zealand.

Europe

The European Association of Urban Missions is a fellowship of city missions across the continent which organises a leaders' conference every three years. It was my privilege to attend one in 1977, held in West Berlin. The Berlin City Mission was celebrating its centenary. Meetings were held nightly in the Kongresshalle, the Berlin seat of government, which holds 3,000 people. One night conference delegates surreptitiously went through checkpoints in the Berlin Wall to attend a meeting in the former headquarters in East Berlin and a large gathering in the Marienkirche.

No one would have thought in April 1989, when the conference was held in Dresden, East Germany, that the Berlin Wall, and all that it represented, would come down so soon. Today there is freedom for the city mission centres in East Berlin. The gospel is preached in the mission halls, but also on the streets and in the homes. Throughout all the years of restriction they have continued their caring ministry to the elderly, the disabled and the needy. There are many such missions in East Germany, as well as in the West.

Likewise, city missions are active in Oslo, Stockholm, Helsinki and many other cities throughout Europe. They differ from missions in other parts of the world in that they are mainly connected with the Lutheran Church, but the aims are basically the same. Staffed by godly Christian workers they prayerfully communicate the love of God in word and deed to the densely populated areas of the urban world.

One of the youngest city missions in Europe is in Madrid—La Mission Evangelica Urbana de Madrid. It was the vision of an Englishman, John Saunders, who is married to a Spanish lady and lives in the city. He invited me to visit him in Madrid in 1983 with a view to surveying the situation to assess the feasibility of starting a city mission. He introduced me to several Christian leaders and the following year arranged for me to do a preaching tour promoting the idea. Later a young lady from Spain spent a year on our Inservice Training Course in Birmingham before returning to join the staff of the new mission. An Englishman who had trained with her returned with her, and later became her husband.

In 1988 I was invited to the first AGM of the Madrid City Mission. It was held in a large Baptist church and was well attended. During my visit I was shown around their mission centre, right in the heart of the city. Needy people queued for admission. A short gospel meeting was followed by personal interviews before clients were issued with clothing vouchers or meal tickets. Voluntary staff worked in the stores exchanging tickets for goods. All was very professionally carried out, and in a spirit of prayer and joyfulness.

The mission organises a number of other activities, including open-air meetings in the main city square which is within walking distance of their central base. Drug addicts and prostitutes are being helped back into society. What a great joy it was to preach in a local church on Sunday and be introduced to a whole family converted to Christ through the new mission. Already the mission is well thought of and supported by a number of different churches of several denominations. Juan Simarro, a teacher, married with a young family but physically disabled, has stepped out in faith to become the director of the new Madrid City Mission.

The ends of the earth

Throughout the years of turmoil in South Africa the Cape Town City Mission has done valiant work, caring for street children, the elderly and needy young people. Racial conflicts have brought great suffering, but this city mission has been involved in rescue work since 1972, providing emergency care and residential homes for victims of all kinds of abuse. Such practical Christian ministry is under the direction of Bruce Duncan, a godly man of faith.

Other cities in Africa have similar works. Letters are regularly received by us from pastors and leaders in that continent expressing their desire to start city missions, receive training or for us to visit them to promote such work.

The great sub-continent of India and Pakistan is also crying out for practical Christian ministry. In Bombay there is now a fine work called the Bombay City Mission. They send out bands of young people to preach, some of whom have taken up residence in Asia's largest slum district to care for people in indescribable poverty. Outreach also takes place in the prostitutes' district. Work in slum areas involves the missionaries in great personal danger.

'The fields are white unto harvest,' is a saying of Jesus which has never been more appropriate than when applied to the cities of our day. Now is the time for Christian men and women to seize the opportunity to reach the cities. The trail has already been blazed. Methods have been proven and skills are available. Surely the command of God to Jonah applies to us today, 'Go to Nineveh [or whatever city] and preach the message that I tell you.'

POST SCRIPT

City Missions in Birmingham, Brighton, Chester, Coventry,
Derby, Edinburgh, Liverpool, Manchester and Swansea have
formed an Association of City Missions to promote:

1 Fellowship between city missions
2 Training programmes in urban evangelism
3 City Mission job opportunities
4 Pooling of ideas and resources
5 National publicity for city mission
6 Public relations for all city missions
7 The founding of new city missions

The Missions can be contacted directly or through the Association
of City Missions, c/o 126 Arden Road, Acocks Green, Birmingham
B27 6AG.

In America the address of the International Union of Gospel
Missions is: 1045 Swift, North Kansas City, MO 64116, USA.

Most of these Missions issue newsletters and magazines and
need prayer and financial support. There are many opportunities
for service, voluntary or paid, short-term or long-term.